4666 T B

Creative Cutting

CREATIVE CUTTING
EASY WAYS TO DESIGN AND MAKE STYLISH
CLOTHES

DIANA HAWKINS

J.M. Dent & Sons Ltd
London and Melbourne

Contents

To Oliver

Designed and produced by
Bellew Publishing Company Limited
7 Southampton Place, London WC1A 2DR

Photographs by Frank Youngs
Diagrams by Ray and Corinne Burrows
Designer: Bob Hook

First published 1986
Text and diagrams © Diana Hawkins 1986
Photographs © Bellew Publishing Co. Ltd 1986

This book is set in Univers by Typesetters Artists and Printers Limited
Printed in Italy by New Interlitho, Milan

J.M. Dent & Sons Ltd
Aldine House, 33 Welbeck Street, London W1M 8LX

British Library Cataloguing in Publication Data
Hawkins, Diana
    Creative cutting.
    1. Dressmaking — Pattern Design
    I. Title
    646.4'3204   TT520
ISBN 0-460-04722-1

Acknowledgments

My thanks are due to a number of people who have helped in the
production of this book: to Ann Sutton for advice and
encouragement from start to finish; to Annette Robinson for
invaluable assistance in making up the garments; to Lene
Walker for her most helpful crosschecking of pattern
instructions; to Keith Biddle at West Sussex College of Design
for his support; to Kennett and Lindsell, Romford, for the use of
dress stands; to the Vilene Organization, Halifax, for supplying
interfacings; to Tootalcraft, Manchester, for sewing threads; to
the Arundel Wool Shop for the use of equipment; and most of all
to Oliver for help in every way.

Note

The cutting diagrams and instructions for the different
bodices, sleeves, yokes and pleats, collars, cuffs, and pockets
are to be found on the pages immediately following the colour
photographs on pp. 32/3, 36/7 and 40/41, 44/45, 48/9 and
52/3, 56/7 and 60/61, 64/5 and 68/9 respectively.

Introduction

At school I was always hopeless at needlework. It seemed to consist of finding the longest, fussiest way of doing things, all tailor tacking and tiny stitches, and the rather shapeless skirts and aprons I finished up with did not make all the effort worthwhile.

When I went on to art school we stopped worrying about neat stitching, and concentrated on being creative instead. In those days colleges were not particularly concerned with professional standards, as they are today, and we got away with throwing ideas together to give an instant fashion-show effect. It was all great fun, but it certainly did not prepare me for earning a living.

It was only when I started working in the London rag trade that I really began to learn, and the shock was dramatic. I remember my first boss tearing my designs into shreds in front of me, screaming at my ignorance. The sample machinists knew most of the answers, but unless you could prove yourself first they were not going to help, and for a long time they seemed the most frightening people on earth

But I was gradually able to pick up the professional ways of doing things. I began to take real pleasure in the way that lines drawn on a piece of pattern card would turn into elegant three-dimensional forms. And I learnt to take pride in cutting a garment from less material than seemed possible, and in finding ways of keeping the cost down in the making. Even the sample machinists became friends, prepared to pass on invaluable tips, and the atmosphere of tight costings, impossible deadlines, and cigar smoke became stimulating rather than terrifying.

Over the years I have never stopped learning. I have found myself designing not just high-fashion clothes but garments of all kinds: children's wear and leisure wear, special outfits for nurses, racing drivers, policewomen . . . In each case what has made the designs work has been the creative use of patterns. And I still marvel at what a designer like Antony Price can achieve by means of inspired cutting.

But you do not have to be a genius, or even a professional, to enjoy the sort of design freedom that good pattern cutting gives you. This book is meant to help people who like making and altering clothes, and who want to go further than someone else's standard pattern bought over the counter.

The basis of the book is a set of pattern blocks, explained in enough detail for you to be able to make your own. Once this is done you have the means of producing any number of different garments, with the book providing suggestions and instructions for a wide variety of collars, sleeves, pockets, and so on. Everything is shown in photographs, in many cases broken down into stages, to make it as easy as possible to follow. I have also included information about the sort of equipment that is likely to be useful, and the various materials, interfacings, and haberdashery you will need.

In the final section I show some finished garments, bringing together a few of the many possible combinations. But these are only a starting point. You will, I am sure, be able to come up with many, many more, reflecting your own individual ideas. That is what creative cutting is about.

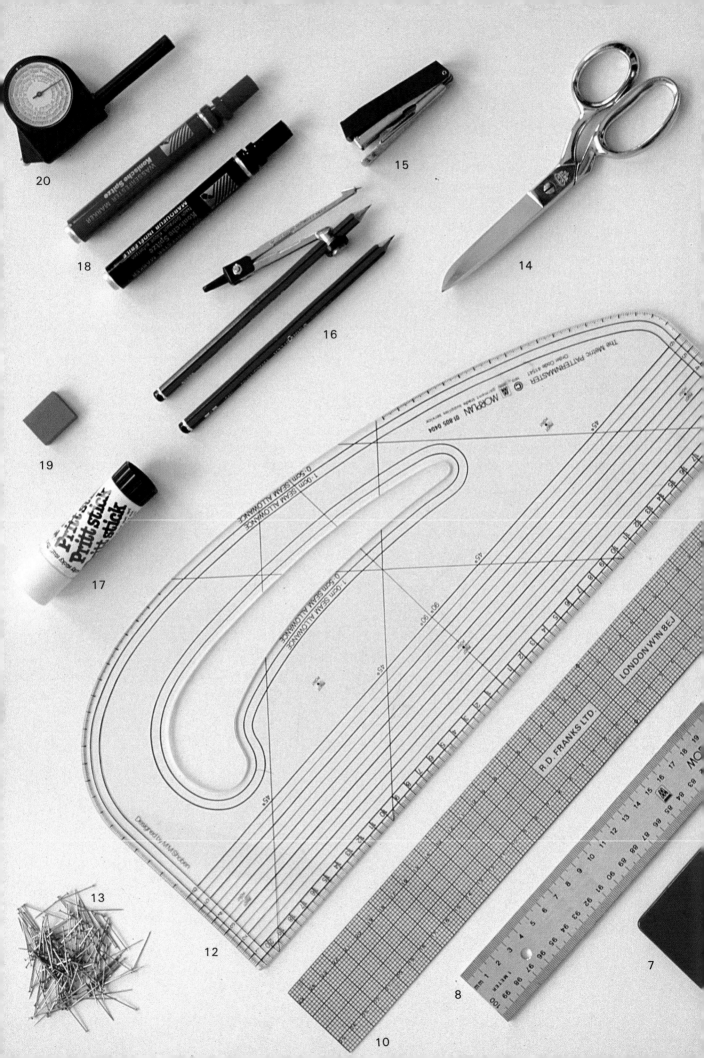

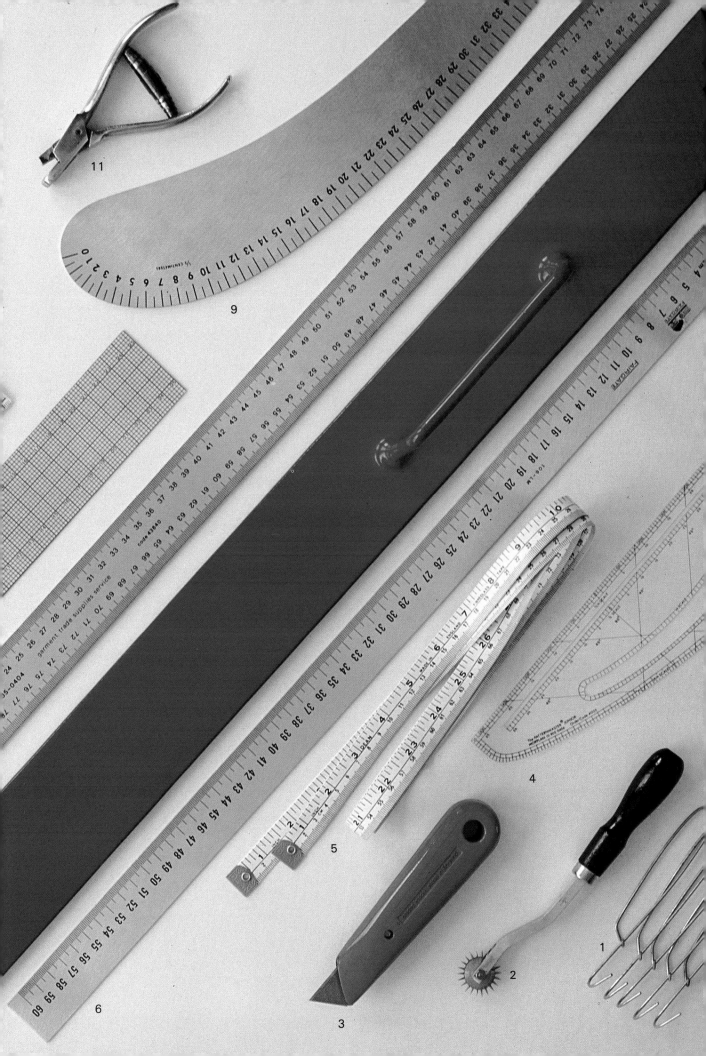

Pattern Cutting Equipment

Do not be put off by the quantity of equipment shown on the previous pages. Some items are essential; others are used mainly by professional pattern cutters. Most of the equipment can be bought from any large haberdasher, but there are also specialist shops such as Franks Ltd, of Kent House, Market Place, London W1, and Morplan, of 56 Great Titchfield Street, London W1. The following notes give a clear indication of which items are essential.

1 Pattern hooks
Useful for hanging up personal blocks in card or thick paper for safe storage.

2 Tracing wheel
Well worth having for transfering a point or line from one pattern piece to another. Also used to trace off the shape of an existing garment without undoing it, by running the tracing wheel through the seams on to the pattern paper (making sure the garment is kept flat).

3 Trimming knife
Useful for cutting lines inside the pattern piece, such as buttonholes, but not essential. Also good for keeping pencils sharp.

4 Small-scale pattern cutting stencil
For designing and drafting 1/4, 1/5, and 2/5 scale diagrams, used in education, and for trying out pattern designs. For the full range of functions see item 12.

5 Tape measure
An essential item, worth having in a good enough quality to resist possible stretching. Those made of fibreglass are the best.

6 Metal metric square
Helpful for drawing accurate right angles, and heavy enough to lie firmly on the paper, but a cheaper, plastic set-square can be used instead.

7 Weight
Used to hold pattern pieces flat and in place while you trace round them. This is very much a professional's item; all sorts of alternatives can be used.

8 Metal metre stick
Well worth having for measuring and drawing long straight lines, and for use in working out *costings*. Cheaper, wooden, metre sticks are also available.

9 Metal curve rule
A useful luxury that facilitates the measurement, drawing, and cutting of smooth curves.

10 Clear plastic graph rule
One of the most useful items, particularly good for adding turning allowances to patterns.

11 Pattern notchers
Used for marking balance points, by snipping small segments from the edge of the pattern piece. If marks are needed in the centre of the pattern piece the paper or card is folded and clipped, leaving a small hole at the required point. Notches can also be made by snipping a V-shape with ordinary scissors.

12 Pattern cutting stencil
A worthwhile specialist tool with a whole range of uses: to measure and draw straight lines; to measure equally either side of a line; to measure curves, by walking the stencil around the curve to be measured; to use as a French curve. The curves on the stencil have been specially designed for pattern cutting, and are ideal for collars, hiplines, hems, etc.; to add seam allowances on to straight lines or curves; to draw lines at 45 degrees for making bias or cross grains; to use instead of a compass.

13 Pins
It is worth buying good-quality pins, which are thinner and sharper, and less liable to snag the fabric than cheaper pins.

14 Scissors/shears
There are numerous varieties of scissors and shears available, at all price levels. It is sensible to have a good-quality pair for cutting fabrics, and a second, cheaper pair for cutting patterns.

15 Stapler
Not essential, but very useful when cutting out a double layer of pattern card or paper, to prevent the layers from slipping. The staples can easily be removed afterwards.

16 Pencils and compass
For drawing lines and curves; pencils can be soft or hard according to preference, but must always be kept sharp.

17 Adhesive stick
Essential. The easiest way to add paper or card to the pattern for alterations or extensions.

18 Marker pens
For clear, durable written information.

19 Eraser

20 Curve measurer
Intended for use with maps, but equally good for taking running measurements around pattern curves, and checking against matching pieces.

Making the Basic Blocks

This process may seem rather complicated, but it is well worth the extra effort necessary to get it right. Once the blocks from the following pages have been constructed to your own personal measurements, it is then possible to cut any number of different designs from them. The basic blocks can be constructed on pattern paper, pattern cutting card, or plain brown wrapping paper. Whatever you use it is important that the blocks should be durable, as they will be put to constant use.

The blocks need to be drafted very accurately, and then used to cut a calico *toile*. When you have made it up, you will see at once if there are any minor adjustments to be made. There will be no seam allowances on the blocks, so these must of course be added when you cut out the calico. Mark it round the block with pencil or chalk, and then add the correct seam allowances, as given below. Never add seam allowances to the block itself, as that would make it much harder to use when creating different designs.

The calico garment, or *toile*, should be machined together using a larger stitch than normal, in a tacking cotton so that it is easy to undo if alterations are needed. Calico is cheap and easily available and has the advantage of keeping its shape well.

How to measure the body
(Diagram p.12)

Bust — Measure the bust at the fullest point.

Waist — Make sure this measurement is comfortable. Then tie a piece of string around the waistline to help take the vertical measurements accurately.

Hips — Measure the widest part of the hips, approximately 21cm (8¼in) from the waistline.

Back width — Measure the back width 15cm (6in) down from the neck bone at the centre back from side seam to side seam.

Chest — Measure the chest 7cm (2¾in) down from the neck point at the centre front, armhole to armhole.

Shoulders — Measure from the neck point to the shoulder bone.

Neck width — Measure a straight line from centre back neck to a point directly below the neck point.

Dart width — A standard measurement (see the chart on page 13, and use the dart width suggested for your own standard size).

Armhole — A standard measurement (see page 13).

Neck to waist — Measure from neck bone at the centre back to the centre back waist.

Armhole depth — A standard measurement (see page 13).

Waist to knee — Measure directly down from the waist to the centre of the kneecap.

Waist to hips — A standard measurement (see page 13).

Top arm — Measure round the arm, bent at a right angle.

Sleeve length — Measure from the shoulder point over elbow to the wrist bone, with your arm bent.

Wrist — This measurement should have a slight *ease*.

Body rise — To take this measurement, sit on a hard chair and measure straight down the side from the waistline to the seat of the chair.

Side seam — Measure straight down the side from the waistline to the floor.

Information to be shown on a pattern
1 The *grain line*
2 Seam allowances
3 Darts and pocket positions
4 Centre line: CF = centre front; CB = centre back
5 Number of pattern pieces to be cut
6 Standard size
7 Balance notches, e.g. at armholes and sleeve heads
8 RSU (right side up), where necessary (see p.76)

Seam allowances Keep to the following seam allowances. Note that the first four on the list have been made very narrow in order to avoid having to clip or trim the seams.

Neck edges	0.5cm (¼in)
Armholes without sleeves	0.5cm (¼in)
Collars	0.5cm (¼in)
Bagged out edges (e.g. the outside edges of cuffs or pockets)	0.5cm (¼in)
Armholes with sleeves	1cm (⅜in)
Sleeve heads	1cm (⅜in)
Attaching cuff edge	1cm (⅜in)
Horizontal seams	1cm (⅜in)
Side seams	1.5cm (⅝in)
Zips	1.5cm (⅝in)
Shoulder seams	1.5cm (⅝in)
Sleeve seams	1.5cm (⅝in)
Standard hem	5cm (2in)

Seams to be joined together should be the same width

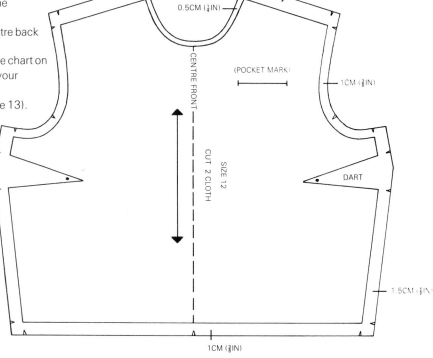

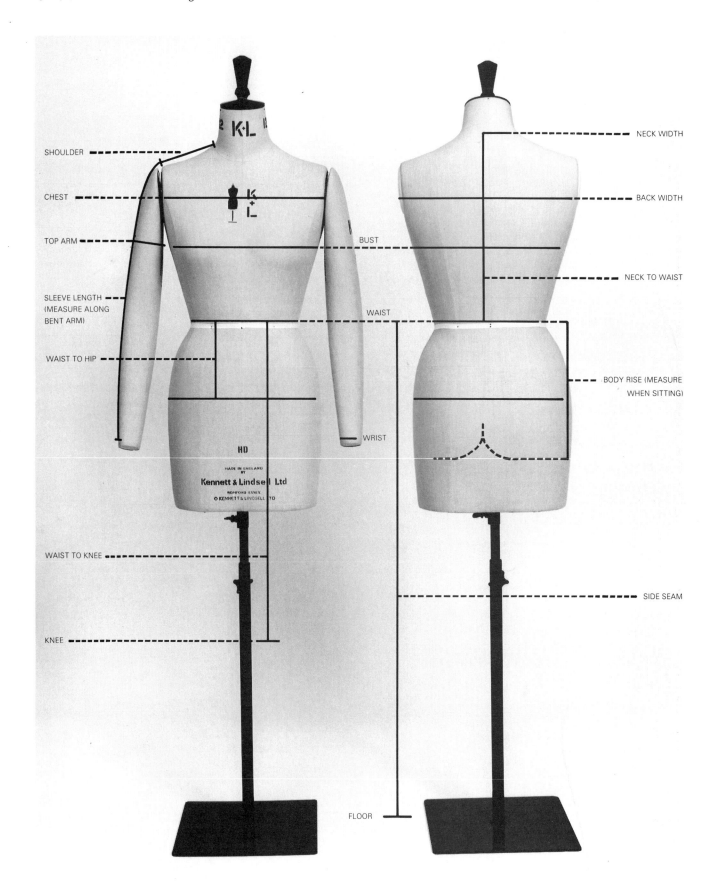

SHOULDER

CHEST

TOP ARM

SLEEVE LENGTH
(MEASURE ALONG
BENT ARM)

WAIST TO HIP

WAIST TO KNEE

KNEE

BUST

WAIST

WRIST

HD

MADE IN ENGLAND
BY
Kennett & Lindsell Ltd
ROMFORD ESSEX
© KENNETT & LINDSELL LTD

NECK WIDTH

BACK WIDTH

NECK TO WAIST

BODY RISE (MEASURE
WHEN SITTING)

SIDE SEAM

FLOOR

Standard Body Measurements in Inches

Size	8	10	12	14	16	18
Bust	$31\frac{1}{2}$	33	$34\frac{1}{2}$	36	38	40
Waist	23	$24\frac{1}{2}$	26	$27\frac{1}{2}$	$29\frac{1}{2}$	$31\frac{1}{2}$
Hips	$33\frac{1}{2}$	35	$36\frac{1}{2}$	38	40	42
Back width	$12\frac{3}{4}$	$13\frac{1}{4}$	$13\frac{1}{2}$	14	$14\frac{1}{2}$	15
Chest	$11\frac{3}{4}$	$12\frac{1}{4}$	$12\frac{3}{4}$	$13\frac{1}{2}$	14	$14\frac{3}{4}$
Shoulder	$4\frac{1}{2}$	$4\frac{3}{4}$	$4\frac{3}{4}$	5	5	$5\frac{1}{4}$
Neck width	$2\frac{3}{4}$	$2\frac{3}{4}$	$2\frac{3}{4}$	3	3	$3\frac{1}{4}$
Dart width	$2\frac{1}{4}$	$2\frac{1}{2}$	$2\frac{3}{4}$	3	$3\frac{1}{4}$	$3\frac{1}{2}$
Armhole	$14\frac{3}{4}$	$15\frac{1}{4}$	16	$16\frac{1}{2}$	17	$17\frac{3}{4}$
Neck to waist	15	$15\frac{1}{4}$	$15\frac{1}{2}$	$15\frac{3}{4}$	16	16
Armhole depth	$7\frac{3}{4}$	8	$8\frac{1}{4}$	$8\frac{1}{2}$	$8\frac{3}{4}$	$8\frac{3}{4}$
Waist to knee	22	$22\frac{1}{2}$	$22\frac{3}{4}$	$23\frac{1}{4}$	$23\frac{1}{2}$	$23\frac{1}{2}$
Waist to hip	$8\frac{1}{4}$	$8\frac{1}{4}$	$8\frac{1}{2}$	$8\frac{1}{2}$	$8\frac{3}{4}$	$8\frac{3}{4}$
Top arm	$9\frac{3}{4}$	$10\frac{1}{4}$	$10\frac{1}{4}$	$11\frac{1}{2}$	12	$12\frac{1}{2}$
Sleeve length	22	$22\frac{1}{4}$	$22\frac{1}{2}$	$22\frac{3}{4}$	23	$23\frac{1}{4}$
Wrist	6	6	$6\frac{1}{4}$	$6\frac{1}{2}$	$6\frac{3}{4}$	7
Bodyrise	$10\frac{1}{2}$	$10\frac{1}{2}$	$10\frac{3}{4}$	11	$11\frac{1}{4}$	$11\frac{1}{2}$
Side seam	40	40	$40\frac{1}{2}$	41	41	$41\frac{1}{2}$

Standard Body Measurements in Centimetres

Size	8	10	12	14	16	18
Bust	80	84	88	92	97	102
Waist	58	62	66	70	75	80
Hips	85	89	93	97	102	107
Back width	32.4	33.4	34.4	35.4	36.6	37.8
Chest	29.8	31.2	32.6	34	35.8	37.6
Shoulder	11.75	12	12.25	12.5	12.8	13.1
Neck width	6.75	7	7.25	7.5	7.8	8.1
Dart width	5.8	6.4	7	7.6	8.2	8.8
Armhole	37.5	39	40.5	42	43.5	45
Neck to waist	38.5	39	39.5	40	40.5	41
Armhole depth	20	20.5	21	21.5	22	22.5
Waist to knee	56	57	58	59	59.5	60
Waist to hip	21	21.25	21.5	21.75	22	22.25
Top arm	25	26	27.5	29	30.5	32
Sleeve length	56	56.5	57	58	58.5	59
Wrist	15	15.5	16	16.5	17	17.5
Bodyrise	26.5	27	27.5	28	28.5	29
Side seam	101	102	103	104	104.5	105

The Bodice Block

The bodice block as shown in diagram A has been constructed using standard size 12 measurements.

You can construct a bodice block to fit yourself by following the procedure set out below, using your own measurements. You will need the following measurements: bust, waist, back width, chest, shoulders, neck width, dart width, neck to waist and armhole depth (see pp. 12—13). The proportions of the diagram will change according to your size but by following the instructions you will be able to produce a block to suit your own shape.

Construction of the outline rectangle
(Points **1**, **4**, **3**, **6**, **5**, and **2**, clockwise on the diagram)
1–2 = armhole depth measurement plus 1.5cm ($\frac{5}{8}$in).
2–3 = half bust measurement plus 5cm (2in).
Square up and down from **3** to give the centre front line.
3–4 = **1–2**. Join up **4** to **1**.
1–5 = neck to waist measurement plus 1.5cm ($\frac{5}{8}$in).
4–6 = **1–5**. Join up **5** to **6**.

Back
1–7 = 1.5cm ($\frac{5}{8}$in).
1–8 = neck width measurement.
Draw in back neck curve from **7** to **8**.
1–9 = 5cm (2in)
To find **10**, square across from **9**, then:
8–10 = shoulder length measurement plus 1cm ($\frac{3}{8}$in)
Draw shoulder line from **8** to intersect the line from **9**.
11 = centre of shoulder line.
11–12, draw a dotted line 5cm (2in) long, sloping 1cm ($\frac{3}{8}$in) towards centre back. Construct dart 1cm ($\frac{3}{8}$in) wide at the top, with the dotted line as the centre line.
2–13 = half back width measurement plus 0.5cm ($\frac{1}{4}$in). Square upwards.
13–14 = half the measurement **2–9**.
15, midway between **2** and **13**.
Square down to **16**, on waistline.

Front
4–17 = neck width measurement less 0.5cm ($\frac{1}{4}$in).
4–18 = 6.5cm (2$\frac{1}{2}$in). Add 0.25cm ($\frac{1}{8}$in) for each size up from size 12.
Draw in front neck curve from **17** to **18**.
3–19 = quarter chest measurement, plus quarter dart measurement.
Square down to **20**, on waistline.
21, bust point, 2.5cm (1in) down from **19**, on a line from **17** through **19**.
17–22 = dart measurement.
Join up **21** to **22**.
10–23 = 1.5cm ($\frac{5}{8}$in).
Square 10cm (4in) across from **23** to **24**.
22–25, draw a line shoulder length from **22**, to intersect the line from **23** to **24** at point **25**.
3–26 = half chest measurement plus half dart.
Square upwards 5cm (2in) from **26**, to **27**.
28, midway between **13** and **26**.
Square down from **28** to **29**, on waistline.
6–30 = 1cm ($\frac{3}{8}$in)
Draw a line from **30** back to **5** (the centre front is always 1cm ($\frac{3}{8}$in) longer than the centre back).
Draw the armhole as shown on the diagram through points **10**, **14**, **28**, **27** and **25**.

Shaping the waist
The waist when darted must measure half the waist plus 2cm ($\frac{3}{4}$in).

Back dart
15–16 is the centre line.
Construct a dart 4cm (1$\frac{1}{2}$in) wide at the waist. Make both sides of the dart the same length.

Side seam
(**28–29**)
Shape 2cm ($\frac{3}{4}$in) at the back side seam at the waist, and 3cm (1$\frac{1}{4}$in) at the front side seam at the waist.

Front dart
21–20 is the centre line.
Construct a dart 5cm (2in) wide at the waist. Make both sides of the dart the same length.

DIAGRAM A

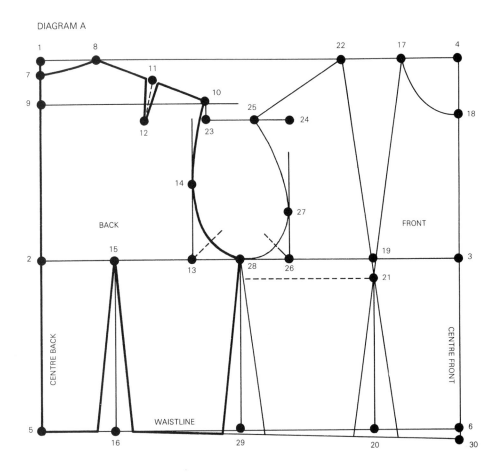

DIAGRAM B

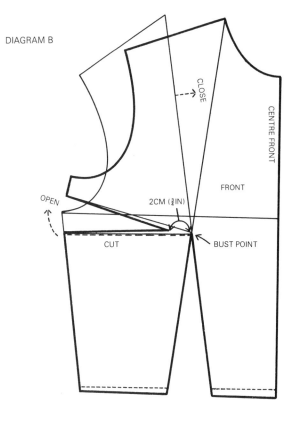

Front bodice block with a new dart position (Diagram B)

The easiest way to construct a front bodice block is to use the bust dart from the neck point.

When designing different shapes from the block it is best to use a side dart.

To change the dart to the side, all you have to do is to cut along a horizontal line from the side seam to the bust point, and close up the neck point dart. The pattern will pivot on the bust point. The dart becomes a side dart, and the fit remains the same. The bust dart must be shortened by 2cm ($\frac{3}{4}$in).

The bodice block is now complete, but remember that there are as yet no seam allowances on it.

The Sleeve Block

The sleeve block is constructed by using the bodice block that has already been made (see pp. 14–15). You will also need the following measurements: armhole, top arm and sleeve length.

Draw a perpendicular line from the horizontal line at the base of the armhole at **1**, touching the front armhole line.
1–2 = one-third of the armhole measurement.
Square across.
3 is halfway between **1** and **2**.
Square across to **4** on the back armhole line.
Continue the line.
1–5 = half of the length of **1–3**.
5A is adjacent to **5**.
6 is the front shoulder point.
5–7 = the measurement of the curve **5–6**, plus 1cm ($\frac{3}{8}$in); join

up with a straight line.
8 is the back shoulder point.
7–9 = the measurement of the curve **4–8**, plus 1cm ($\frac{3}{8}$in); join up with a straight line.
10 is the underarm point on the side seam.
5–11 = the measurement of the curve **5–10**, less 0.25cm ($\frac{1}{8}$in); join up with a straight line.
9–12 = the measurement of the curve **4–10**, less 0.25cm ($\frac{1}{8}$in); join up with a straight line.
11–12 = the top arm measurement, plus approximately 4.5cm ($1\frac{3}{4}$in) ease.
Square down from **7**.
7–13 = sleeve length to wrist.
Square across at **13**.
11–15 is equal and parallel to **12–14**.
14 and **15** are on the horizontal line from **13**.

Sleeve head
Draw a curved line through points **12**, **9**, **7**, **5**, and **11**, as shown in diagram A.
The waistline of the bodice block is the same height as the elbow line.
Draw a curved line through points **14**, **13**, and **15**, as shown in diagram A.

Semi-fitted sleeve
Diagrams B and C.
Trace round the sleeve block. Narrow the sleeve at the wrist by 3cm ($1\frac{1}{4}$in) on each side.
Cut along the back elbow line to the centre sleeve line, and up the centre sleeve line to the elbow line.
Pivot this section towards the front, overlapping 4cm ($1\frac{1}{2}$in) at the hem of the sleeve. This will create an elbow dart. Halve the length of the dart and shorten by 1cm ($\frac{3}{8}$in).
Curve the side seams in 1cm ($\frac{3}{8}$in) at the elbow for slightly more fit (see diagram C).

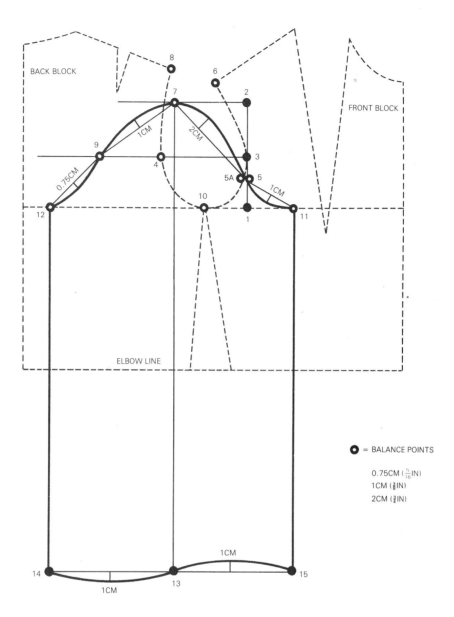

DIAGRAM A

BACK BLOCK

FRONT BLOCK

8

6

7

2

1CM

2CM

9

3

4

0.75CM

5A

5

1CM

10

12

1

11

◉ = BALANCE POINTS

0.75CM ($\frac{5}{16}$IN)
1CM ($\frac{3}{8}$IN)
2CM ($\frac{3}{4}$IN)

ELBOW LINE

1CM

14

13

15

1CM

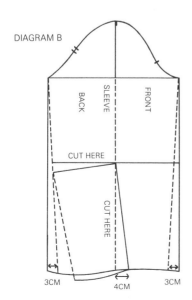

DIAGRAM B

BACK SLEEVE FRONT

CUT HERE

CUT HERE

3CM

4CM

3CM

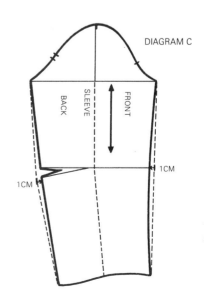

DIAGRAM C

BACK SLEEVE FRONT

1CM

1CM

1CM ($\frac{3}{8}$IN)
3CM ($1\frac{1}{4}$IN)
4CM ($1\frac{1}{2}$IN)

The Skirt Block

You will need the following measurements: waist, hips, waist to hips, skirt length (as required).

Square down and across from **1**.
1–2 = half the hip measurement plus 1.5cm ($\frac{5}{8}$in) for sizes 8–10, 2cm ($\frac{3}{4}$in) for 12-14, and 2.5cm (1in) for 16–18.
1–3 (centre back line) = skirt length.
2–4 (centre front line) = **1–3**.
3–4 = **1–2**.
1–2–3–4 = half the skirt rectangle.
1–5 = waist to hip measurement.
Square across to **6** on the centre front line.

Back

5–7 = one-quarter of the hips measurement plus 1.5cm ($\frac{5}{8}$in). Square down to **8** at hemline.
1–9 = one-quarter of the waist measurement plus 4.25cm (1$\frac{3}{4}$in).
9–10 = 1.25cm ($\frac{1}{2}$in).
Join **10–1** with a dotted line.
Join **9–7** with a dotted line.
Divide the line **1–10** into three parts; mark points **11** and **12** and square down from these points.
11–13 = 14cm (5$\frac{1}{2}$in); **12–14** = 12.5cm (5in).
Construct two darts, each 2cm ($\frac{3}{4}$in) wide, at waist.
Draw in the back waistline in a curve, ending at the centre back with a right angle.
Draw in the side seam, curving it 0.5cm ($\frac{1}{4}$in) outwards.

Front

2–15 = one-quarter of the waist measurement plus 2.25cm ($\frac{7}{8}$in).
15–16 = 1.25cm ($\frac{1}{2}$in).
Join **15–7** with a dotted line.
Join **16–2** with a dotted line.
16–17 = one-third of the length of **2–16**.
Square down from **17**.
17–18 = 10cm (4in).
Construct a dart 2cm ($\frac{3}{4}$in) wide at the waist.
Draw in the front waistline with a curved line.
Draw in the side seam, curving it 0.5cm ($\frac{1}{4}$in) outwards.

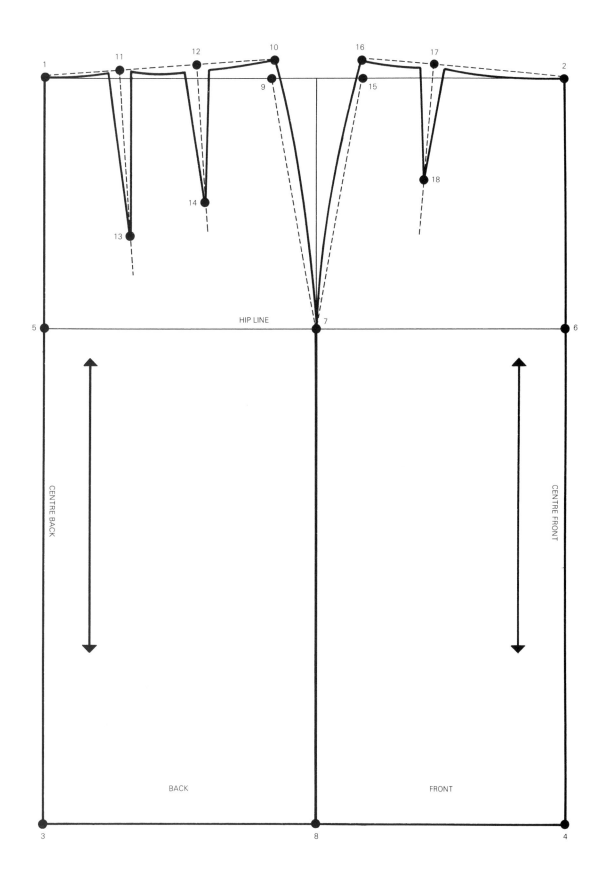

HIP LINE

CENTRE BACK

CENTRE FRONT

BACK

FRONT

The Trouser Block

You will need the following measurements: waist, hips, body rise, side seam, knee width, hem width.

Front

Mark point **1** and square across.

1–**2** = body rise.

Square down and across from **2**.

2–**3** = one-quarter of the hips measurement.

Square up to **4**, on a level with **1**.

3–**5** = one third of **2**–**3**.

Square across to **6**, on the line **1**–**2**.

3–**7** = half of **2**–**3** less 2cm ($\frac{3}{4}$in).

Square up to **8**, on the line **1**–**4**.

8–**9** = the side seam length.

Square down, to give the front crease line.

Square across both ways from **9**.

9–**10** = half **7**–**9** plus 4cm (1$\frac{1}{2}$in).

3–**11** = half of **3**–**7** plus 1cm ($\frac{3}{8}$in).

12 is 0.5cm ($\frac{1}{4}$in) down from **4**.

12–**13** = one-quarter of the waist measurement plus 2.25cm ($\frac{7}{8}$in).

Make a dart from **8**, 2cm ($\frac{3}{4}$in) wide and 10cm (4in) long.

Join **12** to **5**, then **5** to **11** with a curved line, passing at 3.5cm (1$\frac{3}{8}$in) from **3**.

Draw in the curved waistline as shown on the diagram.

9–**14** = half of the hem width less 1cm ($\frac{3}{8}$in).

9–**15** = half of the hem width less 1cm ($\frac{3}{8}$in).

10–**16** = half of the knee width less 1cm ($\frac{3}{8}$in).

10–**17** = half of the knee width less 1cm ($\frac{3}{8}$in).

Join up **14**–**16**–**2**.

Join up **15**–**17**–**11** (slightly curving the line **11**–**17**).

Draw the outline of the front trousers.

Curve the hip line **13**–**6**.

Back

3–**18** = half **3**–**11**.

Square up to **19**, 2cm ($\frac{3}{4}$in) above the hip line, and on to **20** on the waistline.

20–**21** = 0.5cm ($\frac{1}{4}$in).

21–**22** = one-quarter of the waist measurement plus 4.25cm (1$\frac{3}{4}$in).

Join up **21**–**22** horizontally.

Construct two darts, 2cm ($\frac{3}{4}$in) wide and 10cm (4in) long. The inside dart is in the same position as the front dart. The other is midway between the inside dart and the side seam.

11–**23** = half **3**–**11**.

23–**24** = 0.5cm ($\frac{1}{4}$in).

Join up **21**–**19**–**24** with a curved line passing at 3cm (1$\frac{1}{8}$in) from **18**.

19–**25** = one-quarter of the hips measurement plus 1.5cm ($\frac{5}{8}$in).

14–**26**, **15**–**27**, **16**–**28**, **17**–**29**, each = 1cm ($\frac{3}{8}$in).

Draw in the side seam **22**–**25**–**28**–**26**.

Draw in the inside leg **24**–**29** (curved line) and **29**–**27**.

Join up **26**–**27**.

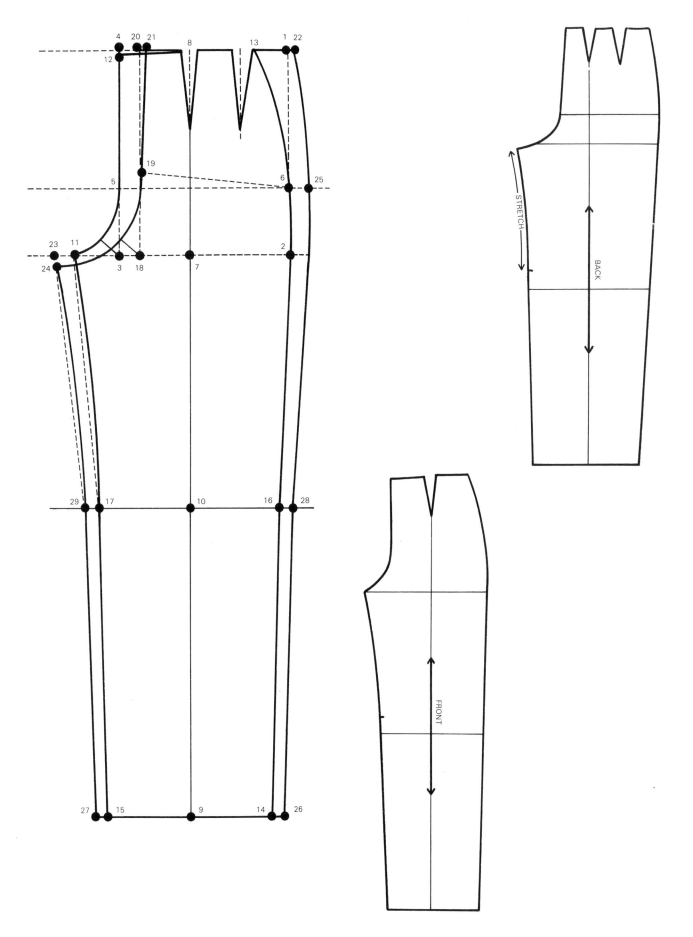

Pattern for trousers with front pleats

(Constructed from the basic trouser block)
Cut down the centre front line and open out 10cm (4in) at waist
(this includes the dart).

Make two pleats at the waist, 6cm (2⅜in) (3cm [1¼in]
finished), and 4cm (1½in) (2cm [¾in] finished).

Narrow the trouser width at the hem. Lower and widen the
trouser crotch as shown.

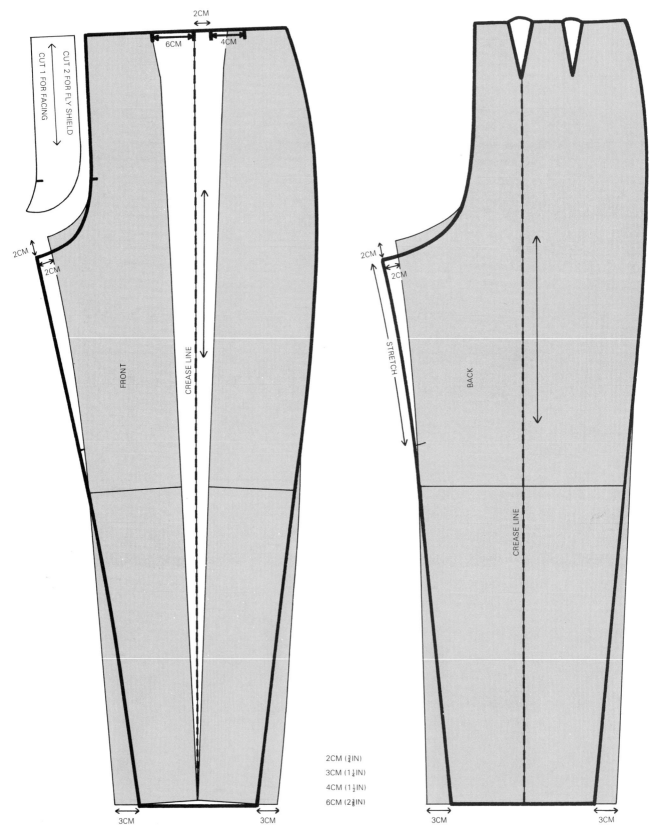

2CM (¾IN)
3CM (1¼IN)
4CM (1½IN)
6CM (2⅜IN)

Pattern for elasticated trousers
(Constructed from the basic trouser block)
These elasticated trousers can be made narrower at the hem by keeping the block together at the hemline (as shown on p.22)

and opening out 10cm (4in) at the hipline. The waistband is cut all in one with the trousers and is folded in half tc carry the elastic.

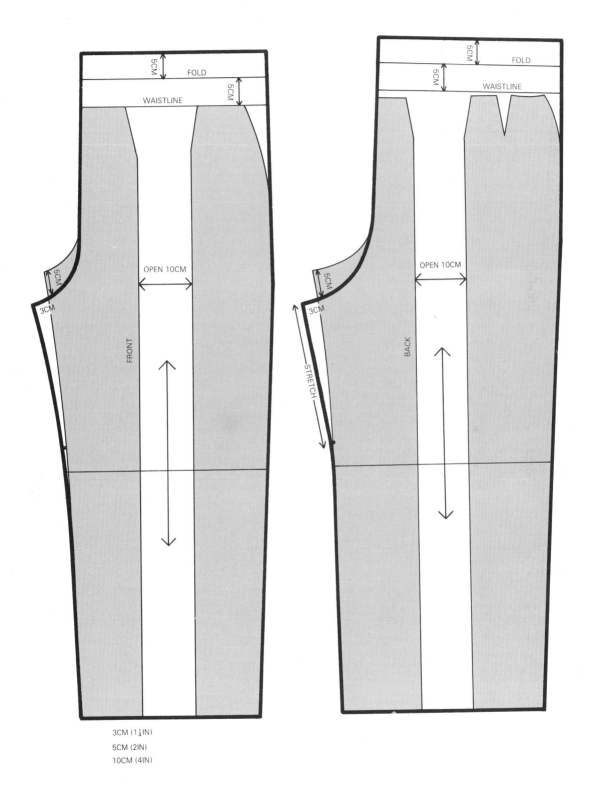

3CM (1¼IN)
5CM (2IN)
10CM (4IN)

Useful Points When Cutting Patterns

1 More often than not the corners of patterns will be right angles, which give a smooth outer edge when the pieces are joined together. Use a set-square to draw the angles.

2 Try to keep all outer lines simple. Always use straight lines or smooth curves.

3 Place back and front curves (such as necklines, armholes and crotch lines) together and draw a smooth, continuous curve.

4 Measure along the fitting line, and not the outer edge of the pattern, if seam allowances have been added.

5 Make sure that seams to be joined together are the same length along the fitting line.

6 Make sure that the side seams hang straight and vertically down the body by balancing up any alterations to front or back measurements.

7 Before slashing up a pattern piece draw a horizontal line across it and number each section to be cut, to avoid confusion later.

8 Hems and turn-ups on tapering or flared garments should be folded up into position before cutting the sides, in order to get the correct angle.

9 Always fold pleats and turn-ups on patterns before cutting the final fitting line. Cut through all the layers and then open out.

10 Mark 'RSU' (right side up) on any pattern pieces that are not reversible.

11 Draw in and cut away yoke seams before changing the rest of the pattern for pleats, gathers, etc.

12 When gathering between two points add 1cm ($\frac{3}{8}$in) extra to the height of the pattern to allow for the gathers.

13 When adding a cuff remember to shorten the sleeve length accordingly.

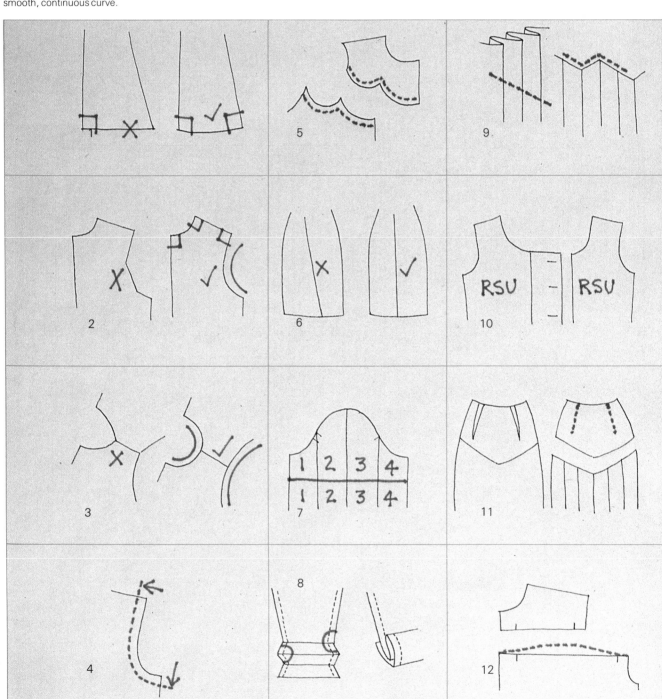

14 Use two notches together to indicate the back of the sleeve head and the corresponding point on the back armhole.

15 Before cutting a raglan sleeve take 1cm ($\frac{3}{8}$in) off the front shoulder seam and add it to the back shoulder seam.

16 When changing the position of a bust dart always swing it from the bust point, and not from the end of the dart.

17 Mark dart points 0.5cm ($\frac{1}{4}$in) in from the end, so that the mark is covered when the dart is sewn.

18 Remember to cut an under collar, under pocket, and under cuff 0.25cm ($\frac{1}{8}$in) smaller on all outer edges than the upper.

19 If an edge is to be bound no seam allowances are needed.

20 When cutting facings make sure that they are the same width where they join, and that their outline is smooth and continuous.

21 Make back neck facings long enough at the centre back for the ends not to be visible from the front neck line.

22 Low necklines should be tightened to avoid gaping. Make a dart in the neckline and then transfer it to the side dart (as shown on p.15). Re-draw the neckline into a smooth curve.

23 Facings must follow the same outline shape as the main pattern to which they will be joined, and must be cut on the same grain.

24 Remember that the human body is a three-dimensional shape. Add fullness all round, not just at the edge of a pattern.

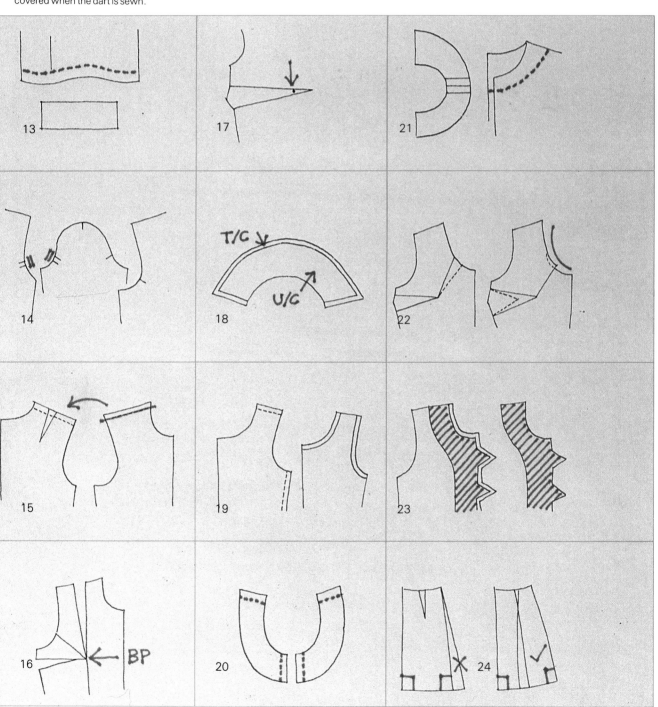

Dartless block constructed from the bodice block

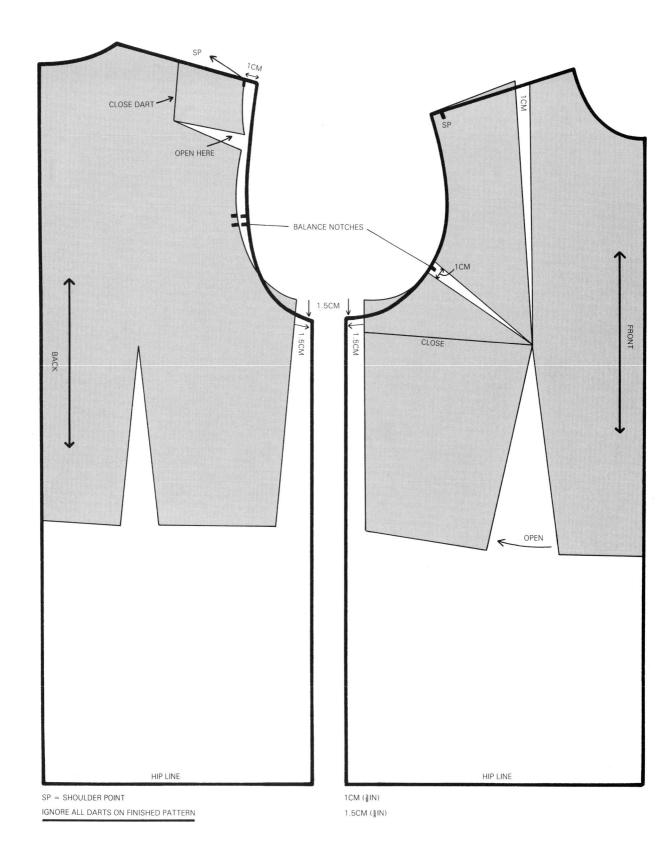

SP = SHOULDER POINT

IGNORE ALL DARTS ON FINISHED PATTERN

1CM (⅜IN)

1.5CM (⅝IN)

Straight sleeve for the dartless block constructed from the sleeve block

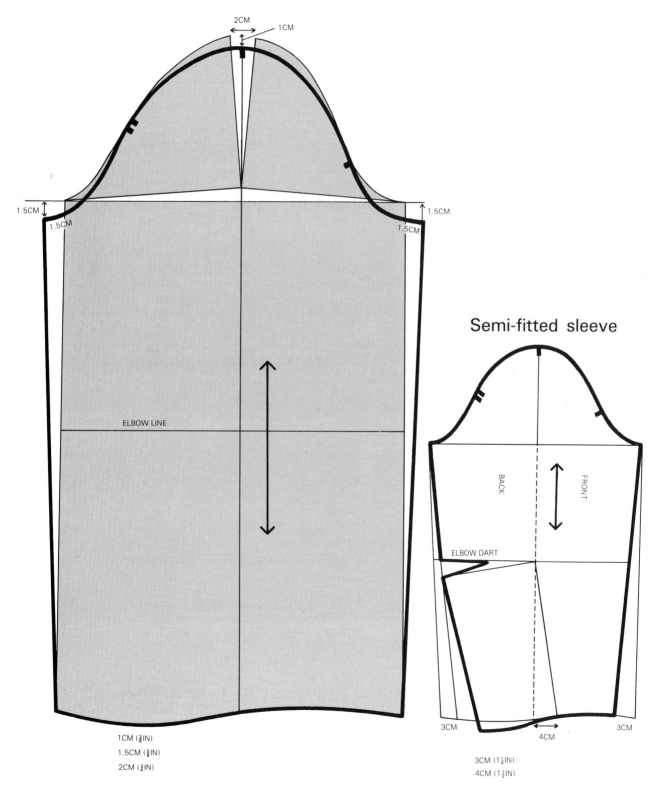

2CM

1CM

1.5CM

1.5CM

1.5CM

1.5CM

ELBOW LINE

1CM (⅜IN)
1.5CM (⅝IN)
2CM (¾IN)

Semi-fitted sleeve

BACK

FRONT

ELBOW DART

3CM

4CM

3CM

3CM (1¼IN)
4CM (1½IN)

The basic bodice sleeveless block

Trace round the basic bodice block. Take 1cm (⅜in) off the shoulder line; raise and tighten the underarm point by 1cm (⅜in). Draw the side seam line down to the normal waist point. Draw a new armhole as shown in the diagram. This is a standard tight-fitting armhole.

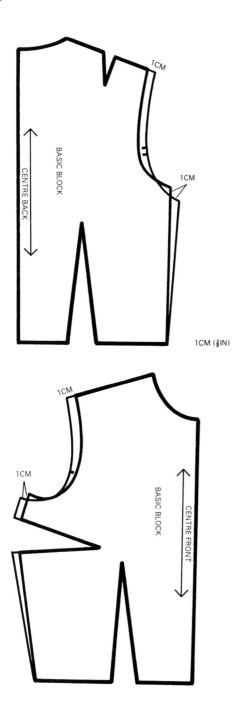

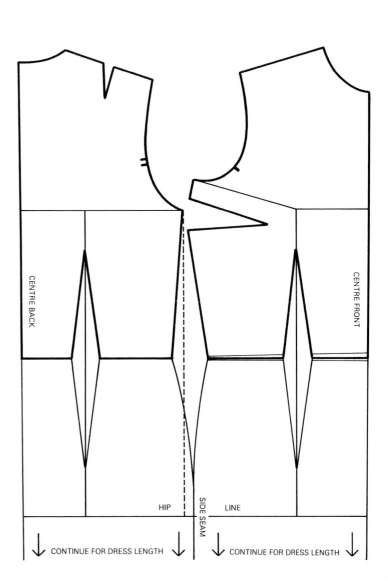

Tight-fitting dress block

Trace round the basic bodice blocks, positioned as shown in diagram A on p.15, but with the new bust dart position from diagram B.

Extend the centre front and centre back lines to the length of dress required and square across.

Draw in the hipline, 21.5cm (8½in) down from the waist. Drop a vertical line from the centre of the hipline to the hemline and draw curved lines up to the side waist points, to become the side seams.

Extend the back and front darts to finish at 7cm (2¾in) above the hipline.

Circular skirts
(Full, half and quarter)
The only measurements required are waist and skirt length.

Full circular skirt
The pattern is based on a quarter segment of the circle (see the diagram). To construct the pattern it is necessary to calculate the radius of the circle at the waist, the circumference of which is the waist measurement.

Circumference = $2\Pi R$, and $\Pi = \frac{22}{7}$ so the simple equation to use to find the radius is as follows:

$$\frac{\text{waist measurement}}{2} \times \frac{7}{22} = \text{radius}.$$

For example, a size 12, 66cm waist works out as:

$$\frac{66}{2} \times \frac{7}{22} = 10.5\text{cm} \left(4\tfrac{1}{8}\text{in}\right) \text{ radius}.$$

Having calculated the radius, draw two sides of a square and mark the radius length on each side, from the corner (point 0 on the diagram). Join the two marks with a compass, centred on 0.

Mark the skirt length points in the same way, measured from the waist mark, not the corner, and draw in the quarter circle. It is possible to use a pencil tied to a length of string pinned to point 0, as an extended compass. Otherwise mark a series of skirt length measurements radiating from the inner segment, to give a guideline for the outer segment.

Mark 'fold' on one edge, and cut out two identical pieces to form the full circular skirt.

Half circular skirt
The pattern is constructed in the same way as the full circular skirt (above), but with the waistline segment marked at *twice* the radius measurement from point 0.

Mark 'fold' on one edge, and cut out one only, to form the complete half circular skirt.

Quarter circular skirt
The pattern is constructed in the same way as the full circular skirt (above), but with the waistline segment marked at *four times* the radius measurement from point 0.

Mark 'single' on one edge, and cut out one only to form the complete quarter circular skirt.

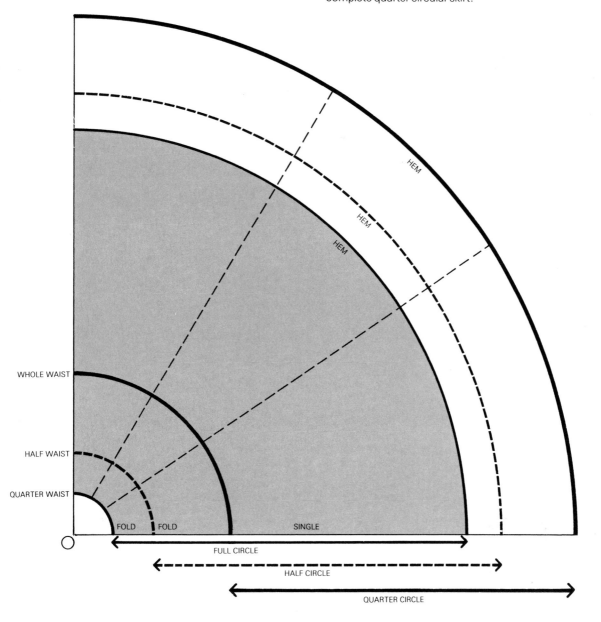

29

Loose fitting bodice block constructed from the dartless block

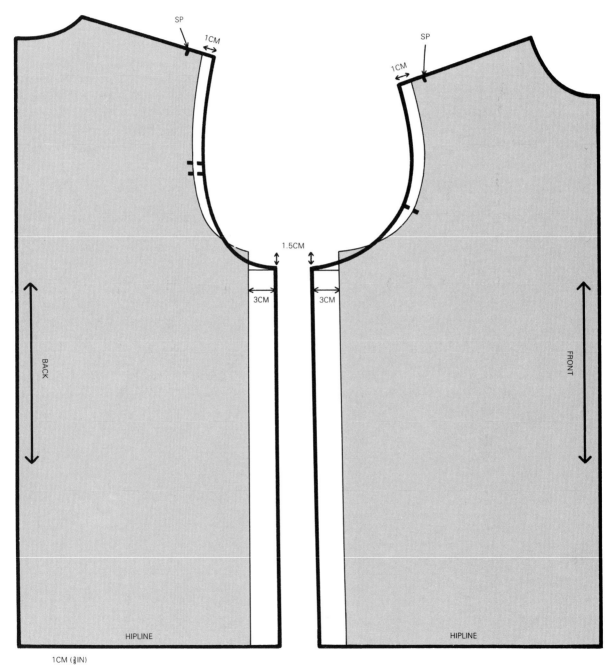

1CM (⅜IN)

1.5CM (⅝IN)

3CM (1¼IN)

Loose fitting sleeve block

(Constructed from the dartless block)

Draw a line 0.75cm ($\frac{5}{16}$in) below the armhole line. Measure the bodice from balance points, and extend the sleeve along this line to fit the bodice requirements.

Join up new the underarm points to the sleeve hem. Lower the sleeve head by 1cm ($\frac{3}{8}$in).

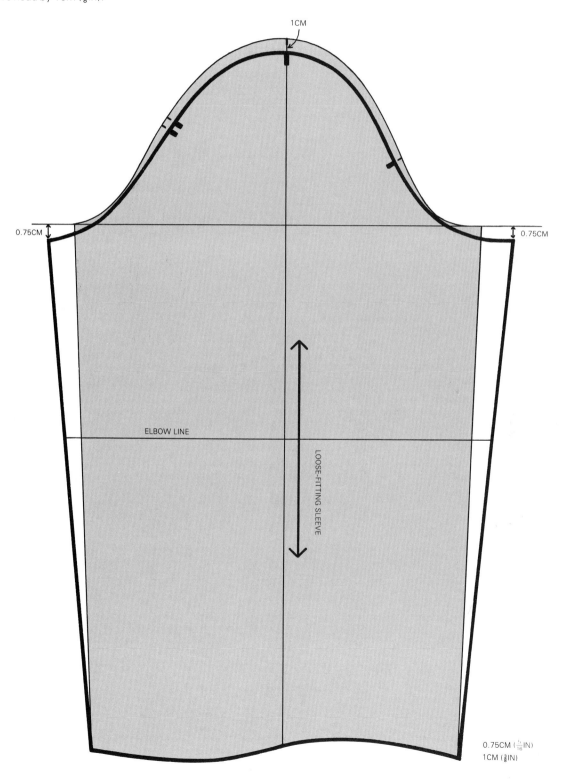

1CM

0.75CM

0.75CM

ELBOW LINE

LOOSE-FITTING SLEEVE

0.75CM ($\frac{1}{16}$IN)
1CM ($\frac{3}{8}$IN)

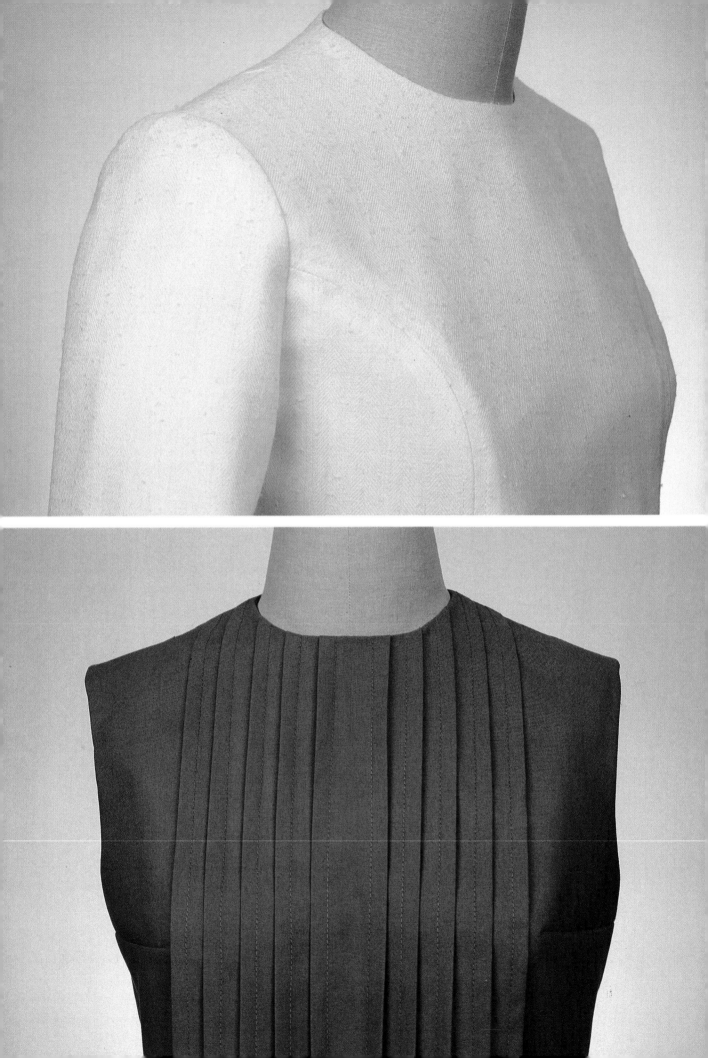

Designing from the Blocks

Size		8	10	12	14	16	18
Elbow	Cm	33	34.5	36	37.5	39	40.5
line	In	13	$13\frac{3}{4}$	$14\frac{1}{4}$	$14\frac{3}{4}$	$15\frac{1}{4}$	16

The following design variations (pp. 32–71) have been constructed on the basis of standard size 12 blocks, but the instructions can be followed for any size.

Certain proportions, such as pocket positions or the depth of a neckline, can of course be adjusted to suit individual requirements.

The one measurement that will need changing for each size is the elbow line, given as 36cm ($14\frac{1}{4}$in) (size 12) in the diagrams, but adjustable as follows:

By making the elbow measurement a set width, it is then possible to have many more variations of sleeves by matching up different top and bottom halves. Sometimes the underarm seams will not form a smooth line when joined. In this case, redraw the underarm seams smoothly, from the underarm point to the wrist.

1CM ($\frac{3}{8}$IN)
2CM ($\frac{3}{4}$IN)

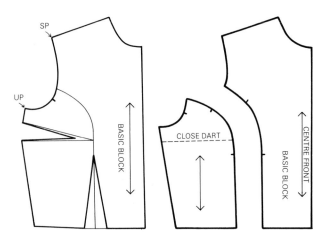

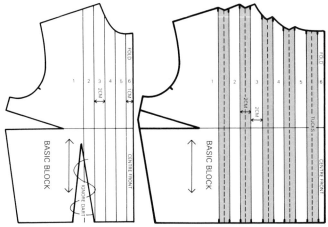

Bust dart in a seam

Use the basic bodice block.

Draw in a new bust shape, starting halfway between the shoulder point and the underarm point on the armhole, and continuing in a curve through the bust point and down the centre of waist dart. Ignore the waist dart unless a completely fitted bodice is required.

Cut along this line, close side dart, and add balance notches along new seam.

Tucked bodice

Use any block. In this diagram the basic block has been used.

Draw five parallel lines down the bodice, the first 1cm ($\frac{3}{8}$in) from the centre front, and the other four 2cm ($\frac{3}{4}$in) apart. Number the sections, and draw a horizontal line across them, through the bust point. Cut out this bodice and cut along the five lines.

Lay these pieces on new paper with a 2cm ($\frac{3}{4}$in) gap between the lines, for the tucks, but keeping the horizontal line straight.

Fold the tucks into position, continuing to the edge of the paper. Lay the block on to the tucked paper and draw round it.

Cut out the final shape with the tucks still folded. Open out the pattern. Ignore the waist dart.

If the dartless or the loose-fitting block is used, the tucks can be extended to the hip line and a *buttonwrap* can be added to the centre front to make it into a blouse (see p.85).

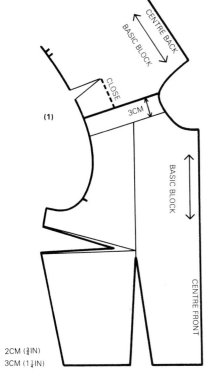

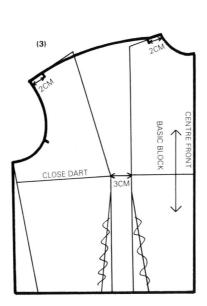

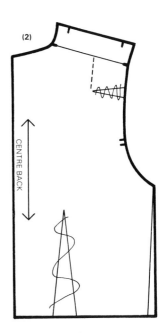

2CM (¾IN)
3CM (1¼IN)

Bust dart changed to gathers (Yoke gathering)

Use any block. In this diagram the basic block has been used.

Place the shoulders together and swing the back shoulder dart into the armhole, by cutting a line at the new dart position to the end of the shoulder dart.

Take 3cm (1¼in) off the front bodice at the shoulder and add 3cm (1¼in) to the back shoulder.

Ignore the back waist dart and straighten the side seam (parallel to the centre back).

Draw and cut a vertical line through the bust point. Open to 3cm (1¼in). Close the side dart. The dart has now moved into the top of the vertical line.

Ignore the waist dart and straighten the side seam (parallel to centre front).

Mark the balance points on the new back and front shoulder line, 2cm (¾in) in. Gather in between these points on the front bodice to fit the back bodice.

Bust dart changed to gathers (Centre front gathering)

Use the basic bodice block.

Draw two horizontal lines, one through the bust point, and one 4cm (1½in) below. Cut out the front bodice; cut along these lines, and close both darts.

Mark the ends of the gathering with notches on the centre front line, 14cm (5½in) from the neck and 9cm (3½in) from the waist. Open out the pattern along the two lines, until the gap between the gathering notches has doubled in length.

The side seam curves slightly but remains the same length.

For making up (not shown), gather the fronts separately and then join them together. The centre front line must be its original length.

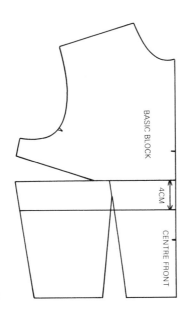

4CM (1½IN)
9CM (3½IN)
14CM (5½IN)

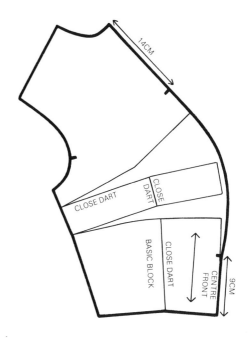

Strapped sleeve head

Use the basic sleeve block.

Trace round the sleeve. Draw a strap 3cm (1¼in) wide, and divide into four sections.

Take 2cm (¾in) ease from the sleeve head. Cut up the strap lines and the centre line and open out. Raise the sleeve head 4cm (1½in). Trace round the new sleeve shape.

This sleeve should not be cut on the *bias*.

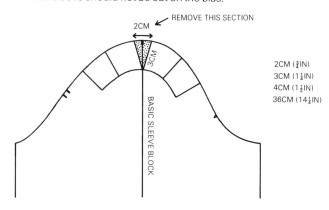

2CM (¾IN)
3CM (1¼IN)
4CM (1½IN)
36CM (14¼IN)

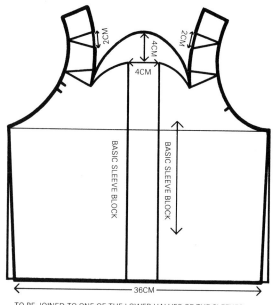

TO BE JOINED TO ONE OF THE LOWER HALVES OF THE SLEEVES
FROM pp. 56–63

Leg-of-mutton sleeve

Any sleeve block can be used. This diagram is based on the dartless block.

Cut down the centre line of the sleeve to the elbow line. Cut across. Open out 22cm (8⅝in) at the sleeve head, making sure that the elbow line measures 36cm (14¼in).

Add 1cm (⅜in) to the sleeve head and take 1cm (⅜in) off the shoulder length. This brings the sleeve head back to the SP (shoulder point).

Raise the sleeve head 5cm (2in) more. Draw in the new sleeve head. Mark notches at the end of the gathering, and corresponding notches on the armhole, 7cm (2¾in) down from the SP.

This sleeve can be cut on the bias, as in the photograph, or on the straight of grain. Note: if you are cutting on the bias, make sure that the bottom half of the sleeve can also be cut on the bias.

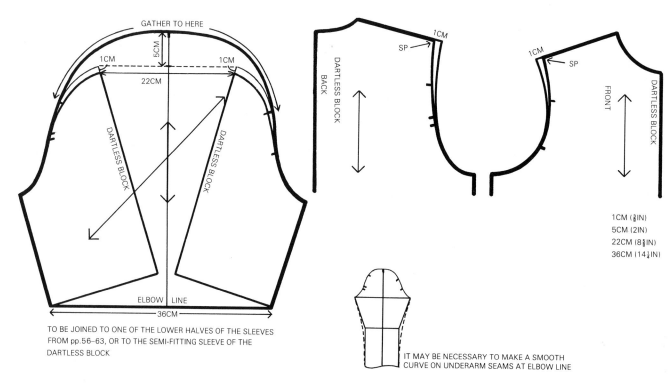

1CM (⅜IN)
5CM (2IN)
22CM (8⅝IN)
36CM (14¼IN)

TO BE JOINED TO ONE OF THE LOWER HALVES OF THE SLEEVES
FROM pp.56–63, OR TO THE SEMI-FITTING SLEEVE OF THE
DARTLESS BLOCK

IT MAY BE NECESSARY TO MAKE A SMOOTH
CURVE ON UNDERARM SEAMS AT ELBOW LINE

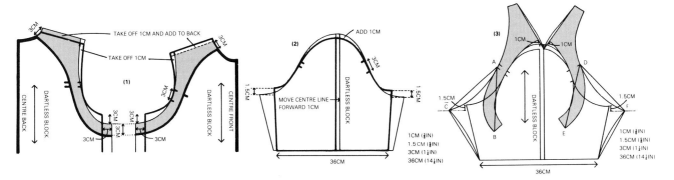

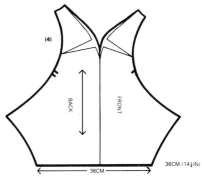

Loose-fitting low raglan with square shoulder

Use the dartless block.

Take 1cm ($\frac{3}{8}$in) off the front shoulder line, and add 1cm ($\frac{3}{8}$in) to the back shoulder line, to bring the balance of the garment forward.

Take the armhole back to the shoulder point, and add 1cm ($\frac{3}{8}$in) to the crown of the sleeve head. Lower and widen the armhole by 3cm ($1\frac{1}{4}$in) each way.

Move the front balance point up 3cm ($1\frac{1}{4}$in) on the armhole and sleeve.

Sleeve — Draw a line 1.5cm ($\frac{5}{8}$in) below the armhole line. Measure the bodice from the balance points, and extend the sleeve along this line to fit the bodice measurements.

Move the centre line forward 1cm ($\frac{3}{8}$in).

Place sections on the sleeve, matching the balance points as for a high raglan.

Mark points A, B, C, D, E, and F. Draw a line 1.5cm ($\frac{5}{8}$in) below the armhole line. A–B = A–C, D–E = D–F.

Join with curves. Curve the sleeve seam to the elbow line.

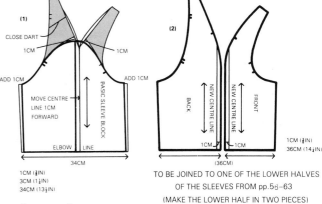

TO BE JOINED TO ONE OF THE LOWER HALVES
OF THE SLEEVES FROM pp.56-63

To square the shoulder — Cut a line parallel with the neck at the shoulder point, and swing it open by the depth of the shoulder pad, and slightly raise the shoulder lines. If a two-piece sleeve is required, follow the instructions for a high raglan (below).

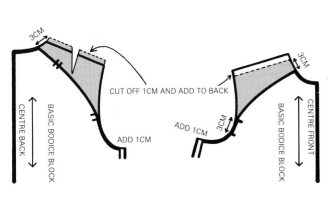

Two-piece high raglan sleeve

Any block can be used as long as the sleeve head is at the shoulder point (alter if necessary). In this diagram the basic block has been used, and 1cm ($\frac{3}{8}$in) has been added to the sides of the sleeve and bodice.

Take 1cm ($\frac{3}{8}$in) off the front shoulder line and add 1cm ($\frac{3}{8}$in) to the back shoulder line, to bring the balance of the garment forward.

Make a new balance point on the front armhole, 3cm ($1\frac{1}{4}$in) up. Draw in a raglan line on the back and front bodice. Cut away

these sections.

Draw the centre line 1cm ($\frac{3}{8}$in) towards the front on the sleeve. Place sections on sleeve, matching the balance points. Shoulder points are 1cm ($\frac{3}{8}$in) above the sleeve head.

Close the back shoulder dart. Trace round the outline, curving the shoulder seam and continuing it into the new centre line of the sleeve.

Cut out the sleeve and cut along the new sleeve line. Add 1cm ($\frac{3}{8}$in) on each half along this line, curving it into the shoulder seam.

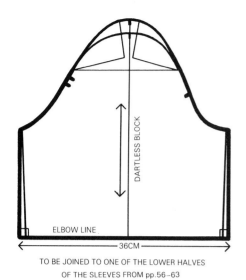

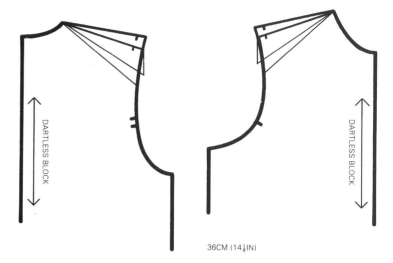

TO BE JOINED TO ONE OF THE LOWER HALVES
OF THE SLEEVES FROM pp.56–63

36CM (14¼IN)

Padded square shoulder

Use the basic block or the dartless block.

Trace round the bodice and sleeve blocks. Slash up the bodice from armhole to neck. Open the depth of shoulder pad. Cut across the sleeve head and up the centre line, and open out by as much as has been added to the armhole.

Add 1cm ($\frac{3}{8}$in) to the side seams at the elbow line, to make 36cm (14¼in) width.

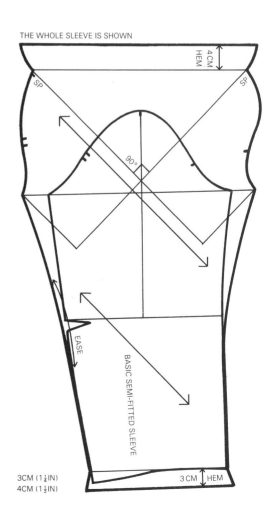

Draped sleeve

This is a full-length sleeve. Use the basic semi-fitted sleeve block.

Draw round the top part of block, and down to 13cm (5⅛in) on the side seams. Cut out and cut down the centre line. Draw the whole of the sleeve block, and lay the two halves of the first sleeve on top of it, so that the underarm points are on the same line and there is a 90-degree angle in the centre.

Draw a line from SP to SP. Add a 4-cm (1½-in) hem, curving the ends to correspond with the sleeve head. Join the new underarm points to the elbow with a slightly curved line. Straighten the sleeve hem to eliminate most of the elbow dart. Ease the rest in. Add 3cm (1¼in) to the hem.

This sleeve must be cut on the bias.

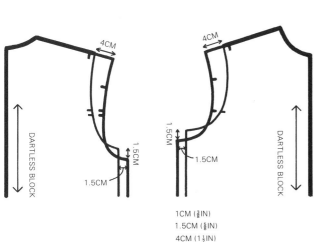

GATHER

DARTLESS BLOCK

ELBOW LINE

DARTLESS BLOCK

ELBOW LINE

36CM

36CM (14¼IN)

TO BE JOINED TO ONE OF THE LOWER HALVES
OF THE SLEEVES FROM pp.56–63

Gathered sleeve head

Trace round the chosen sleeve block.

Divide the sleeve head into five sections above the back balance point. Mark balance points for gathers, at the top of sections **1** and **5**. Cut up the sections and open out as shown in diagram. Make a smooth line at the bottom of sections **1** and **5**.

Add 1cm (⅜in) to each side seam at the elbow line, to make 36cm (14¼in) width.

This sleeve can be cut on the straight of grain or on the bias.

IT MAY BE NECESSARY TO MAKE
A SMOOTH CURVE ON UNDERARM
SEAMS AT ELBOW LINE

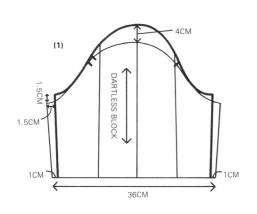

(1)

4CM

DARTLESS BLOCK

1.5CM

1.5CM

1CM

1CM

36CM

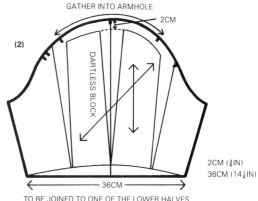

GATHER INTO ARMHOLE

2CM

(2)

DARTLESS BLOCK

2CM (¾IN)
36CM (14¼IN)

36CM

TO BE JOINED TO ONE OF THE LOWER HALVES
OF THE SLEEVES FROM pp.56–63

Dropped shoulder with gathered sleeve head

Any block can be used. This diagram is based on the dartless block.

Lower the sleeve head 4cm (1½in) and widen, and drop the sleeve side seam by 1.5cm (⅝in). Add 1cm (⅜in) to each side seam at the elbow line to make 36cm (14¼in) width.

Add 4cm (1½in) to the shoulder seams, and widen and drop the bodice side seams by 1.5cm (⅝in). Re-position the balance points.

Divide the sleeve into four, and open up for gathers. Raise the sleeve head 2cm (¾in). Mark notches to show where the gathering stops, both on the sleeve and on the armhole.

This sleeve can be cut on the straight of grain or on the bias.

4CM

4CM

DARTLESS BLOCK

1.5CM

1.5CM

1.5CM

1.5CM

DARTLESS BLOCK

1CM (⅜IN)
1.5CM (⅝IN)
4CM (1½IN)

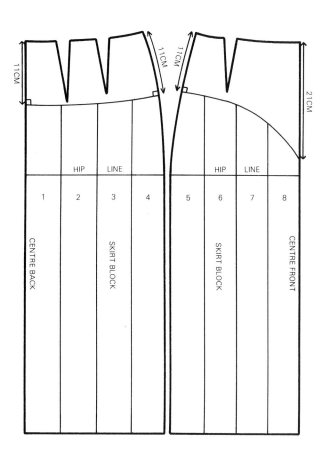

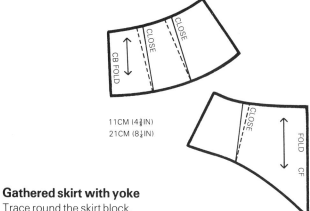

11CM (4⅜IN)
21CM (8¼IN)

Gathered skirt with yoke

Trace round the skirt block.

Mark the depth of the yoke, and draw in the yoke line as shown on the diagram. Cut the yoke off and close up the darts. The yoke pieces should lie flat.

Divide the remaining back and front skirt into sections, with parallel lines. Number the sections, and make sure the hipline is drawn in.

Cut into strips and open out, so that the skirt now measures twice its original width. This is called 'two to one' gathering.

If a fuller skirt is required, open out the pattern so that the skirt measures three times its original width. This is called 'three to one' gathering.

Draw a curved line at top of skirt, just below the highest points on **6** and **7**. Extend the skirt rectangles to the required length.

The zip is located in the side seam. (See p.105 for information on gathers.)

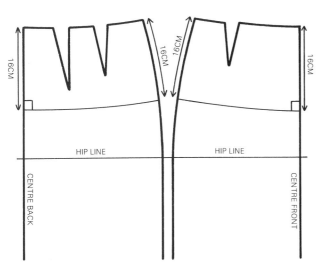

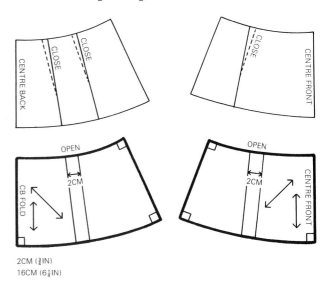

2CM (¾IN)
16CM (6¼IN)

Basque of the top

Trace round the top half of the skirt block. Draw a line across the block, 16cm (6¼ in) down from the waistline. This line will be slightly curved. Make sure that it hits the centre front and centre back at right angles.

Cut off these sections and close the darts. Open out 2cm (¾ in) back and front through the centre of the basque.

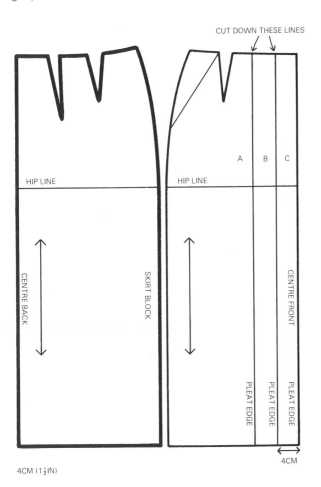

4CM (1½IN)

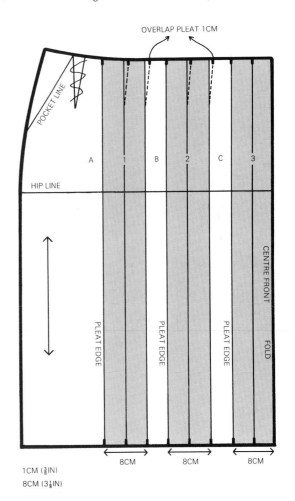

1CM (⅜IN)
8CM (3⅜IN)

Skirt with front pleats

Trace round the skirt block.

This skirt has three knife pleats on either side of the centre front, facing inwards. The 4-cm (1½-in) pleats each require an extra 8cm (3⅜ in) to fold under. Cut round the front skirt and down the lines marked for the pleats. Leave an 8-cm (3⅜-in) gap between each piece and at the centre front.

Ignore the dart in the front block, transferring its width to pleats **1** and **2** by overlapping them at the waist by 1cm (⅜ in) each.

The same can be done on the back skirt if necessary. (See pp. 96-97 for information on pleats.)

Rever collar

Trace round the chosen front bodice. Mark in the front button wrap 1.5cm ($\frac{5}{8}$in). Extend the shoulder line.

1–2 = 2cm ($\frac{3}{4}$in); **3** is the break point.

Draw a line from **3** through **2** to **4**.

2–4 = back neck measurement plus 1cm ($\frac{3}{8}$in).

4–5 = 2cm ($\frac{3}{4}$in), **2–4** = **2–5**.

Square a line across at right angles to the line **5–2**.

5–6 = 2.5cm (1in), **6–7** = 6.5cm ($2\frac{1}{2}$in).

Draw a line from **6** parallel to the line **5–2**, hitting the shoulder line at 0.75cm ($\frac{5}{16}$ in) to the left of **1**. Continue the line, and curve into the neckline.

Draw in the outer collar and rever. Fold back along the breakline to see if it is the right shape. Trace off the collar. Mark balance points on the neck and collar.

Cut, and mould the under collar with an iron. Then cut the top collar using the under collar as a pattern, but with 0.25cm ($\frac{1}{8}$in) extra on the outer edge.

The rever facing should also have 0.25cm ($\frac{1}{8}$in) extra on the outer edge, or 0.5cm ($\frac{1}{4}$in) if the fabric is thick. (See p.106 for making up a rever collar.)

Peter Pan collar

Draw a new neckline on the chosen block, as shown. Overlap the shoulder seams 2cm ($\frac{3}{4}$in) at the shoulder point, starting at the new neckline.

Draw in a collar of the desired width, dropping 0.75cm ($\frac{5}{16}$ in) at the centre front. Trace off the collar. The under collar must be 0.25cm ($\frac{1}{8}$in) smaller than the top collar. Cut facings. (See p.111 for making up a Peter Pan collar.)

0.75CM ($\frac{1}{16}$IN)
2CM ($\frac{3}{4}$IN)
5CM (2IN)

Shirt collar with fly front

Place the shoulders of the chosen block together, and lower front neckline by 1.5cm ($\frac{5}{8}$in).

The button wrap is 1.5cm ($\frac{5}{8}$in). For a fly front for this size button wrap add 10cm (4in) beyond the wrap.

The collar

Construct a rectangle **1–2** by **1–3**,

1–2 = half of neck measurement

1–3 = 10cm (4in)

Point **4** is at three-quarters the length **1–2**.

2–5 = 0.75cm ($\frac{5}{16}$in)

1–6 = 4cm (1$\frac{1}{2}$in)

Square across to **7**.

7–8 = 0.75cm ($\frac{5}{16}$in)

Draw outline of collar **3–8**.

5–9 = 1.5cm ($\frac{5}{8}$in), *buttonstand*.

Draw in stand.

6–10 = 0.75cm ($\frac{5}{16}$in)

Shape a line from **10** to the vertical line from **4**.

Trace the collar and stand.

Mark a buttonhole and notches.

(See p.104 for making a fly front, and p.107 for making a shirt collar.)

Cowl collar

Any block can be used.

Draw a line 4cm (1$\frac{1}{2}$in) in from SP (shoulder point), to reach the centre front line 3cm (1$\frac{1}{4}$in) below the bust point. Divide this section into three and open up, so that the centre front measures half the length again, with the point of section **3** now being 45 degrees to the edge.

Make two pleats on the shoulder seam, 2cm ($\frac{3}{4}$in) on the double. Add a 3cm (1$\frac{1}{4}$in) neck facing. This will be a straight line.

The cowl must be cut on the bias, and should be cut out in calico first to ensure that the pleats are at the correct angle.

There is a separate back neck facing. The shoulder seams of the facings must be the same length.

(See p.108 for making up a cowl collar.)

2CM ($\frac{3}{4}$IN)
3CM (1$\frac{1}{4}$IN)
4CM (1$\frac{1}{2}$IN)

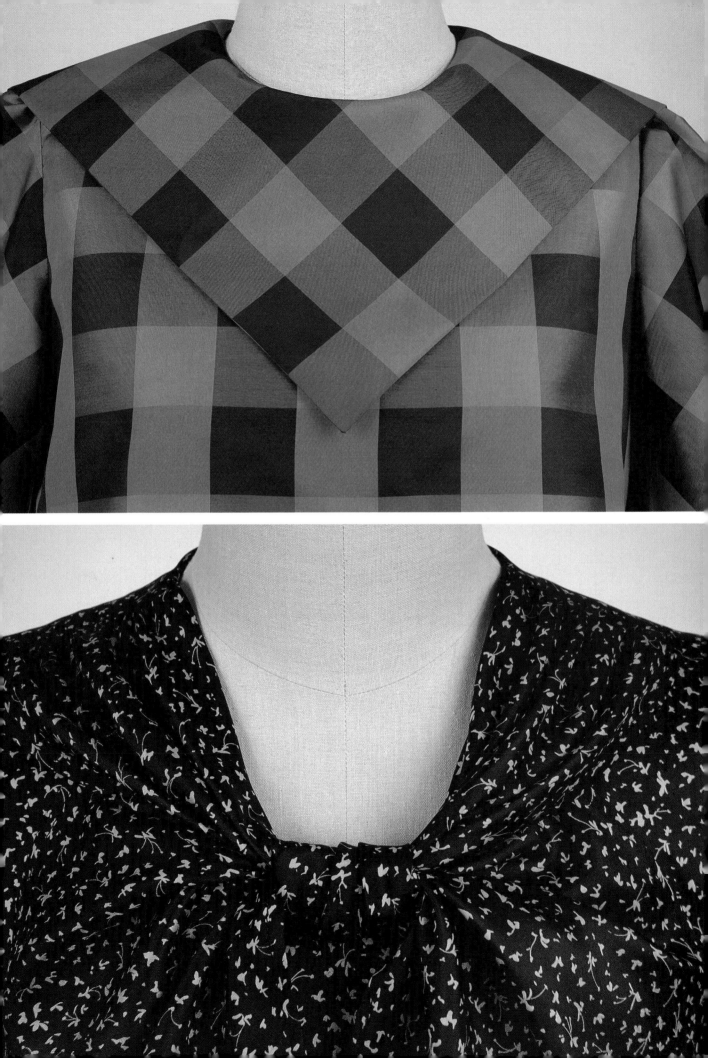

Frill collar

Use any bodice block for this collar, but only use the dartless block for this sleeveless armhole.

Lower the neckline 4cm (1½in) all round. Draw a circle that measures the same as the whole neckline. Then draw an outer circle the width of the frill from the first. Mark a seam.

Cut six circles. Make a crossway binding the length of the neckline (see pp.94-5).

For the sleeveless armhole, follow the diagram and cut facings to fit the new armhole shape.
(See p.109 for making up a frill collar.)

Note: to cut a flounced circular collar without gathering, make the circumference of the inner circle one third of the whole neckline. Draw a new outer circle the width of the frill from the inner one. Cut six circles, and continue as with a frill collar (above).

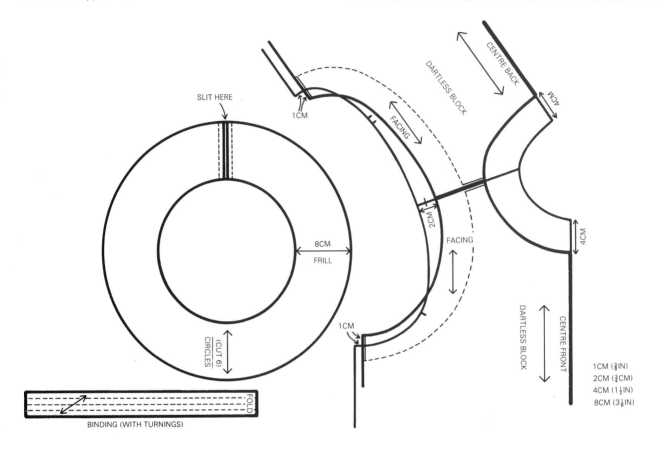

Shawl collar

Use any block.

Mark buttonholes and add a *buttonstand* (see p.85). Extend the front shoulder line. Draw a line from the break point to 2cm (¾in) along the extended shoulder line.

Place the back bodice, reversed, at the neck point of the front bodice. Swing the back so that the outer shoulder point overlaps the extended line by 8.5cm (3⅜in). Draw round the top half of the back block.

Draw in the roll line and the outer edge of the collar, as shown in diagram.

Trace off facing, which is also top collar. This top collar is cut on the fold and on the bias, at the centre back, with 0.5cm (¼in) added to the outer edge. The facing has a seam below the collar.
(See p.110 for making up a shawl collar.)

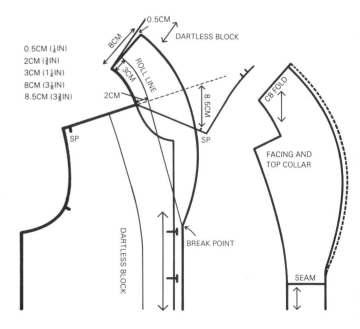

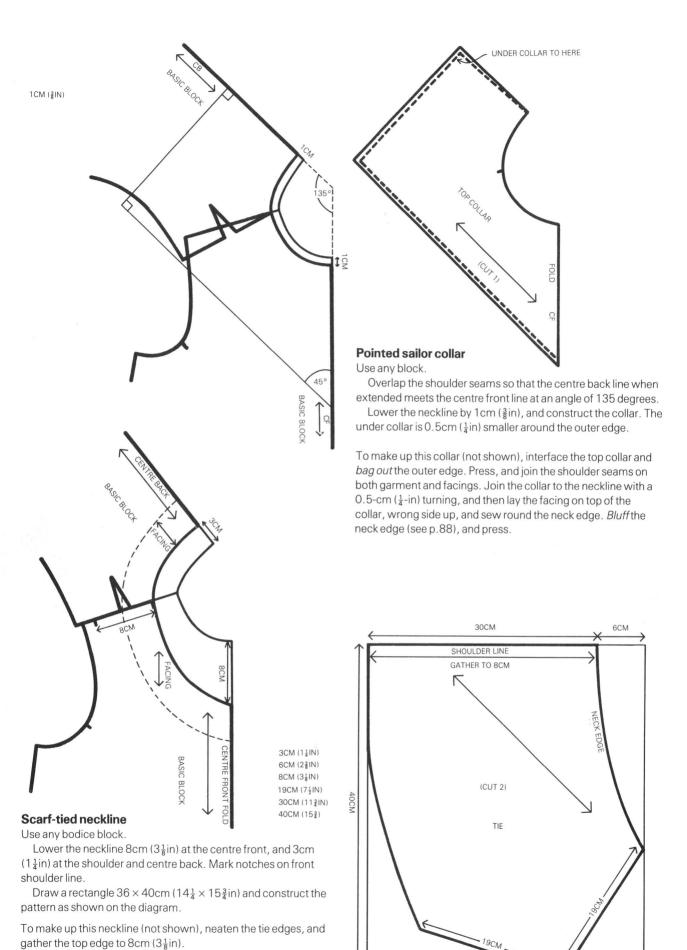

Pointed sailor collar

Use any block.

Overlap the shoulder seams so that the centre back line when extended meets the centre front line at an angle of 135 degrees.

Lower the neckline by 1cm ($\frac{3}{8}$in), and construct the collar. The under collar is 0.5cm ($\frac{1}{4}$in) smaller around the outer edge.

To make up this collar (not shown), interface the top collar and *bag out* the outer edge. Press, and join the shoulder seams on both garment and facings. Join the collar to the neckline with a 0.5-cm ($\frac{1}{4}$-in) turning, and then lay the facing on top of the collar, wrong side up, and sew round the neck edge. *Bluff* the neck edge (see p.88), and press.

Scarf-tied neckline

Use any bodice block.

Lower the neckline 8cm ($3\frac{1}{8}$in) at the centre front, and 3cm ($1\frac{1}{4}$in) at the shoulder and centre back. Mark notches on front shoulder line.

Draw a rectangle 36 × 40cm ($14\frac{1}{4}$ × $15\frac{3}{4}$in) and construct the pattern as shown on the diagram.

To make up this neckline (not shown), neaten the tie edges, and gather the top edge to 8cm ($3\frac{1}{8}$in).

Attach along the front shoulder lines. Machine the shoulders together and face the neck edge.

3CM ($1\frac{1}{4}$IN)
6CM ($2\frac{3}{8}$IN)
8CM ($3\frac{1}{8}$IN)
19CM ($7\frac{1}{2}$IN)
30CM ($11\frac{3}{4}$IN)
40CM ($15\frac{3}{4}$)

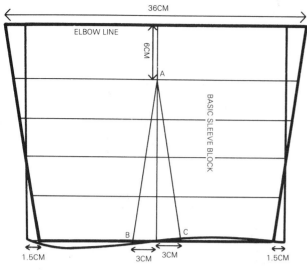

Ruched sleeve

Use the basic sleeve block. Lengthen the elbow line to 36cm (14¼in). Narrow the bottom of the sleeve by 1.5cm (⅝in) at either side and straighten the hemline.

Mark point A 6cm (2⅜in) down the centre line.

Cut out triangle A,B,C. Slice along the four horizontal lines to sleeve seam, and open out with a 4-cm (1½-in) gap on the centre line. Add a 3-cm (1¼-in) hem. Draw round the new shape.

This sleeve should not be cut on the bias.

For making up the sleeve (not shown), gather the curved edges to 18cm (7in), and then sew them together, continuing into the sleeve hem.

Press the seam open carefully. Sew the sleeve seam, and catch up the hem.

1.5CM (⅝IN)
3CM (1¼IN)
4CM (1½IN)
6CM (2⅜IN)
18CM (7IN)
36CM (14¼IN)

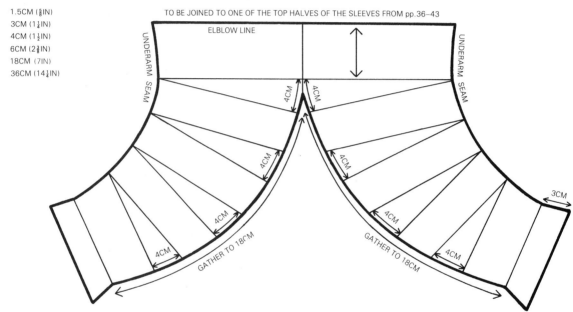

TO BE JOINED TO ONE OF THE TOP HALVES OF THE SLEEVES FROM pp.36–43

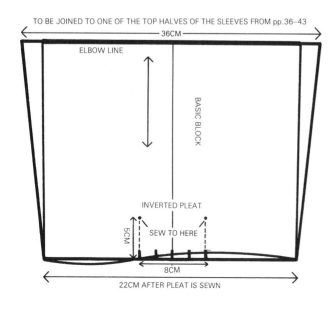

TO BE JOINED TO ONE OF THE TOP HALVES OF THE SLEEVES FROM pp.36–43

Sleeve with a pleat

Any sleeve block can be used, as long as the elbow line measures 36cm (14¼in). In this diagram the basic sleeve block has been used.

Mark an inverted pleat on a straightened bottom of the sleeve. The pleat is sewn up 5cm (2in). Mark these points.

This sleeve should not be cut on the bias.

(See p.123 for making up a sleeve with a pleat.)

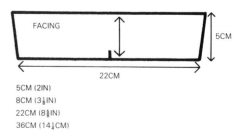

5CM (2IN)
8CM (3⅛IN)
22CM (8⅝IN)
36CM (14¼CM)

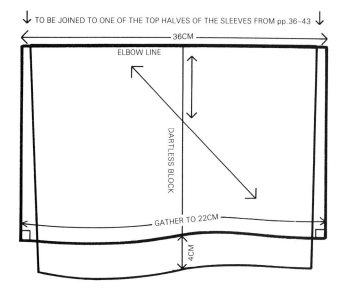

↓ TO BE JOINED TO ONE OF THE TOP HALVES OF THE SLEEVES FROM pp.36–43 ↓

Turned-back shaped cuff

Any sleeve block can be used, as long as the elbow line measures 36cm (14¼in). In this diagram the dartless sleeve block has been used.

Drop vertical lines down from the ends of the lengthened elbow line. Shorten the sleeve by 4cm (1½in).

This sleeve can be cut on the bias or on the straight grain (as in the sample).

(See p.119 for making up a turned-back shaped cuff.)

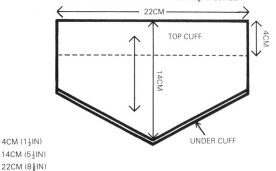

THE TOP CUFF BECOMES THE UNDER CUFF WHEN TURNED BACK
MAKE THE OLD UNDER CUFF 0.25CM (⅛IN) LONGER

4CM (1½IN)
14CM (5½IN)
22CM (8⅝IN)
36CM (14¼IN)

1.5CM (⅝IN)   6CM (2⅜IN)
2CM (¾CM)   11CM (4⅜IN)
3CM (1¼CM)   20CM (7⅞IN)
4CM (1½CM)   36CM (14¼IN)
5CM (2IN)

↓ TO BE JOINED TO ONE OF THE TOP HALVES OF THE SLEEVES FROM pp.36–43 ↓

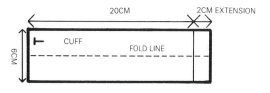

Cuff with an opening in the side seam

Any sleeve block can be used, as long as the elbow line measures 36cm (14¼in). In this diagram the dartless sleeve block has been used.

Shorten the sleeve by 1.5cm (⅝in) for a 3-cm (1¼-in) wide cuff (always allow 1.5cm [⅝in] extra in the length when there is a tight cuff). Take 3cm (1¼in) off each side of the sleeve.

Gather the centre of the sleeve only. Place a notch 5cm (2in) up the side seam for the opening.

This sleeve can be cut on the bias (as in the diagram), or on the straight of grain. The cuff is shown in the diagram.

(See p.121 for making up a cuff with an opening in the seam.)

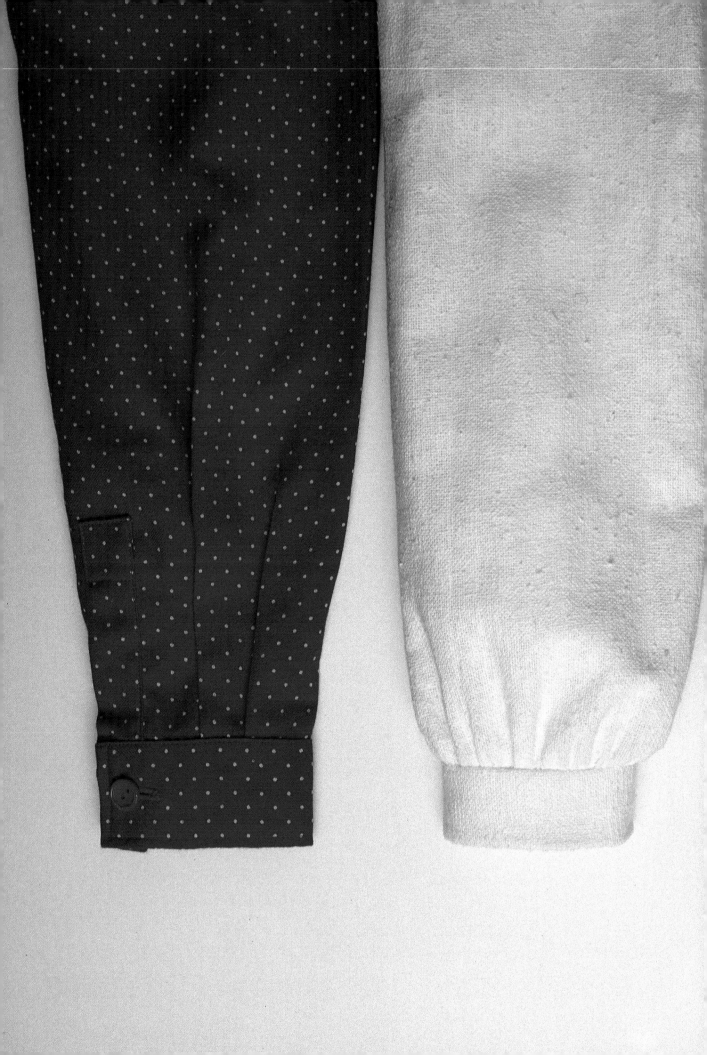

TO BE JOINED TO ONE OF THE TOP HALVES OF THE SLEEVES FROM pp.36–43

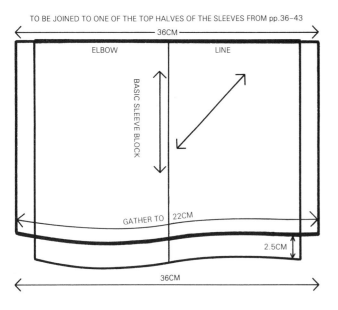

36CM

ELBOW   LINE

DARTLESS BLOCK

PLEAT   PLEAT   PLEAT
2CM   4CM   4CM

Shirt cuff with placket

Use any sleeve block. Lengthen the elbow line to 36cm (14$\frac{1}{4}$in).

Mark the placket opening 8cm (3$\frac{1}{8}$in) long, halfway between back seam and centre line.

Place three pleats, as shown in the diagram, along the bottom of the sleeve. The finished width must be 21cm (8$\frac{1}{4}$in). The extra 1cm ($\frac{3}{8}$in) is for the seam allowance either side of the placket.

The cuff is 22cm (8$\frac{5}{8}$in) long, 2cm ($\frac{3}{4}$in) of which is attached to the placket.

This sleeve must be cut on the straight of grain.

(See p.120 for making up a shirt cuff with placket.)

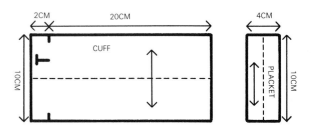

2CM   20CM   4CM

CUFF   10CM   PLACKET   10CM

2CM ($\frac{3}{4}$IN)
4CM (1$\frac{1}{2}$IN)
10CM (4IN)
20CM (7$\frac{7}{8}$IN)
36CM (14$\frac{1}{4}$IN)

TO BE JOINED TO ONE OF THE TOP HALVES OF THE SLEEVES FROM pp.36–43

36CM

ELBOW   LINE

BASIC SLEEVE BLOCK

GATHER TO   22CM

2.5CM

36CM

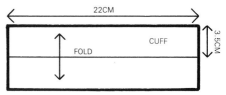

22CM

FOLD   CUFF   3.5CM

2.5CM (1IN)
3CM (1$\frac{1}{4}$IN)
3.5CM (1$\frac{3}{8}$IN)
22CM (8$\frac{5}{8}$IN)
36CM (14$\frac{1}{4}$IN)

Cuff without an opening

Any sleeve block can be used, as long as the elbow line measures 36cm (14$\frac{1}{4}$in). In this diagram the basic sleeve block has been used.

Widen the sleeve to 36cm (14$\frac{1}{4}$in) and shorten it by 2.5cm (1in) to allow for the cuff. The cuff is a rectangle a 22 × 7cm (8$\frac{5}{8}$ × 2$\frac{3}{4}$in).

This sleeve can be cut on the straight of grain or on the bias.

(See p.118 for making up a cuff without an opening.)

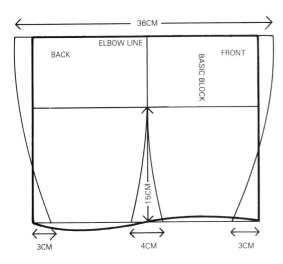

36CM

ELBOW LINE

BACK

FRONT

BASIC BLOCK

15CM

3CM 4CM 3CM

Sleeve with button and loop

Use any sleeve block. In this diagram the basic sleeve block has been used.

Lengthen the elbow line to 36cm ($14\frac{1}{4}$in).

Make the hem of the sleeve narrower by 10cm (4in), as shown in the diagram. Mark a point 15cm (6in) up the centre sleeve line. Draw curved lines from this point to the narrowed sleeve hem, and from the lengthened elbow line to the sleeve hem. Divide in two.

Mark a notch up the centre lines for a 7-cm ($2\frac{3}{4}$-in) opening. The double notch on the diagram is for the rouleau position.

The facings are as shown.

This sleeve can be cut on the straight of grain or on the bias. (See p.122 for making up a sleeve with button and loop.)

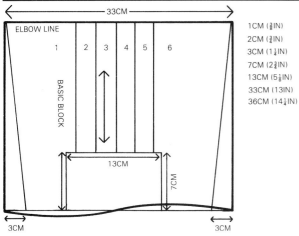

33CM

ELBOW LINE

1 2 3 4 5 6

BASIC BLOCK

13CM

7CM

3CM 3CM

1CM ($\frac{3}{8}$IN)
2CM ($\frac{3}{4}$IN)
3CM ($1\frac{1}{4}$IN)
7CM ($2\frac{3}{4}$IN)
13CM ($5\frac{1}{8}$IN)
33CM (13IN)
36CM ($14\frac{1}{4}$IN)

Sleeve with mock cuff

Use any sleeve block. In this diagram the basic sleeve block has been used.

Narrow the hem width by 3cm ($1\frac{1}{4}$in) on each side. Straighten the hemline.

Divide the sleeve up as shown in the diagram, and cut out the rectangle. Cut up and open out sleeve 10cm (4in) at the base, and at the elbow line until it measures 36cm ($14\frac{1}{4}$in). Cut up and close the hem of the rectangle by 3cm ($1\frac{1}{4}$in). Mark the rouleaux positions on this piece.

The facing for the sleeve hem is cut in one piece.

This sleeve can be cut on the straight of grain or on the bias.

For making up the sleeve (not shown), gather the base to 13cm ($5\frac{1}{8}$in). Interface the rectangle, make the *rouleaux*, and attach

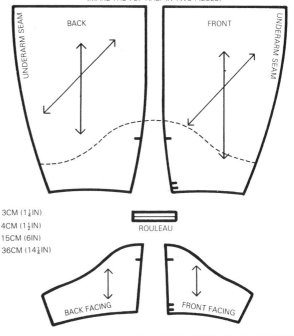

TO BE JOINED TO ONE OF THE TOP HALVES OF THE SLEEVES FROM pp.36–43
(MAKE THE TOP HALF IN TWO PIECES)

UNDERARM SEAM

BACK

FRONT

UNDERARM SEAM

3CM ($1\frac{1}{4}$IN)
4CM ($1\frac{1}{2}$IN)
15CM (6IN)
36CM ($14\frac{1}{4}$IN)

ROULEAU

BACK FACING

FRONT FACING

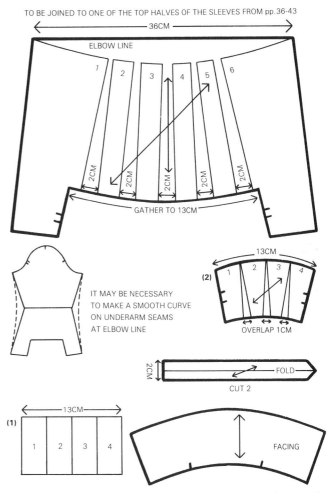

TO BE JOINED TO ONE OF THE TOP HALVES OF THE SLEEVES FROM pp.36–43

36CM

ELBOW LINE

1 2 3 4 5 6

2CM 2CM 2CM 2CM 2CM

GATHER TO 13CM

IT MAY BE NECESSARY TO MAKE A SMOOTH CURVE ON UNDERARM SEAMS AT ELBOW LINE

13CM

(2) 1 2 3 4

OVERLAP 1CM

2CM FOLD

CUT 2

(1) 13CM

1 2 3 4

FACING

these to the rectangle at the sides. Tie the *rouleaux* in a bow, and insert the complete section into the sleeve.

Sew up the sleeve seam and the facing seam. Sew on the facing, *bluff* (see p.88) the edge and catch up inside by hand.

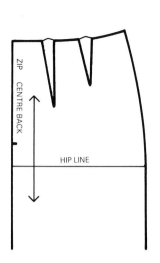
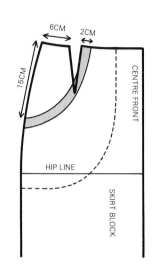
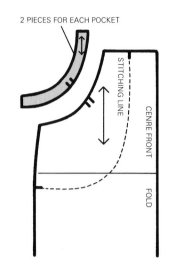
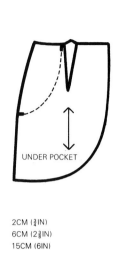

Curved pocket with contrast edge

(Single pocket bag stitched to skirt)
Use the skirt or trouser block. Follow the directions shown in the diagrams.

For making up the pocket (not shown), interface both layers of contrast strips, and overlock the lower edge of the inside one.

Sew them together along the outer edge, and *bluff* (see p.88).

Attach the top contrast strip to the garment, right sides together, and sink stitch the under strip through this seam line (for sink stitching, see p.95).

As there is no top pocket bag, the under pocket, which has a dart in it, is topstitched to the garment. Sew the pocket in with the side seam and the waist seam.

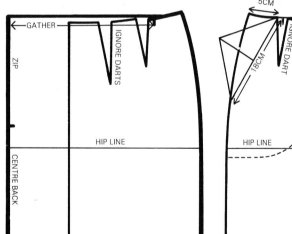
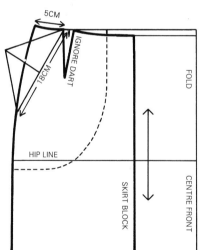
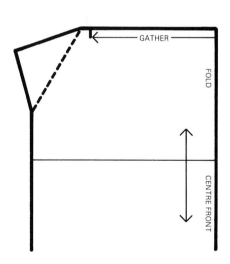

Skirt pocket with flap

Use the skirt block or trouser block.

Add 12cm (4¾in) to the centre front and centre back for gathering, and ignore the darts. Follow the directions shown in the diagrams.

For the top pocket put an extra 0.25cm (⅛in) on outer edge of flap.

For making up this pocket (not shown), interface the top pocket flap to 2cm (¾in) past the fold line. *Bag out* the pocket flap and topstitch with two rows. Sew the top and under pockets together around the bag. Sew the pocket in with the side seam and the waist seam.

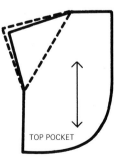
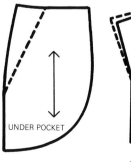

5CM (2IN)
18CM (7IN)

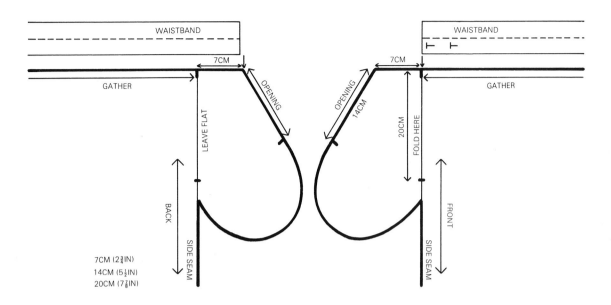

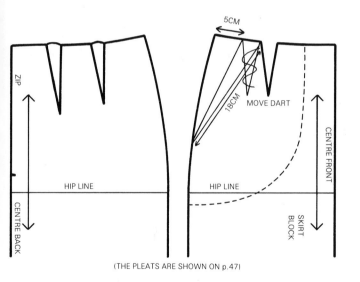

(THE PLEATS ARE SHOWN ON p.47)

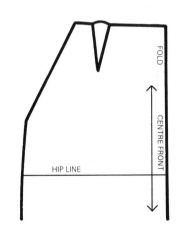

5CM (2IN)
18CM (7IN)

Pocket and opening combined

This pocket and opening can be used on a skirt or gathered trousers, and no block is needed.

Follow the directions shown on the diagrams. To achieve a balanced look it is best to have a pocket at each side, rather than only one.

(See p.117 for making up a pocket and opening combined.)

Trouser pocket

Use the trouser block, or the skirt block with the front dart moved forward 2cm (¾in).

Follow the directions as shown on the diagrams.
(See p.116 for making up the trouser pocket.)

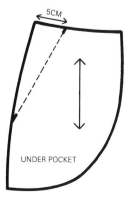

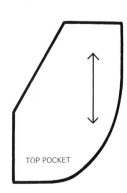

These four pocket patterns have seam allowances added on the diagrams.

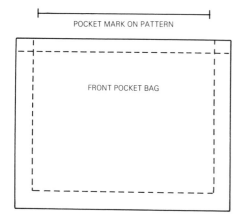

POCKET MARK ON PATTERN

FRONT POCKET BAG

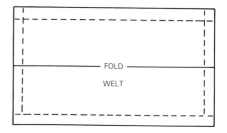

FOLD

WELT

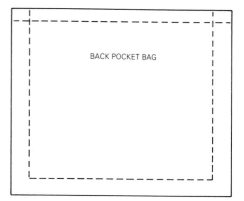

BACK POCKET BAG

Welt pocket

Mark the position of the pocket 0.5cm ($\frac{1}{4}$in) up from the base of the welt.

The welt and the top of the pocket bag should have 0.5-cm ($\frac{1}{4}$-in) turnings, with 1-cm ($\frac{3}{8}$-in) turnings elsewhere. The front pocket bag is 1cm ($\frac{3}{8}$in) shorter than the back.

When used as a breast pocket, the welt should measure 10×3cm ($4 \times 1\frac{1}{4}$in).

POCKET MARK ON PATTERN

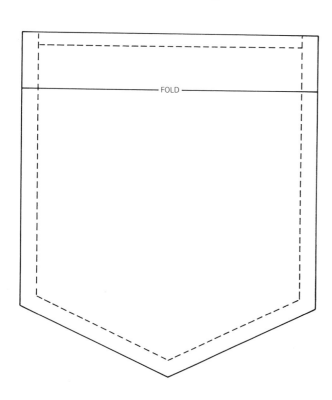

FOLD

Patch pocket

Mark the position of the pocket at the top edge, just inside the pocket width, so that the marks are covered by the pocket. There is a 0.5-cm ($\frac{1}{4}$-in) turning at the top hem, and 1-cm ($\frac{3}{8}$-in) turnings on the outer edges.

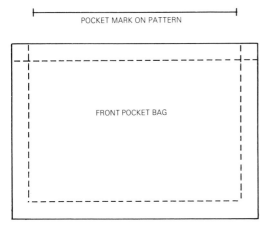

POCKET MARK ON PATTERN

FRONT POCKET BAG

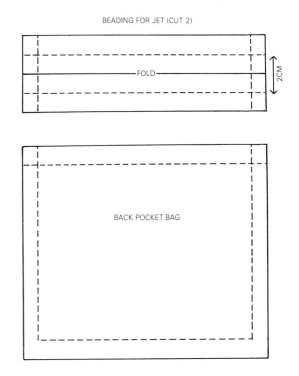

BEADING FOR JET (CUT 2)

FOLD

2CM

BACK POCKET BAG

Jet pocket

Mark the position of the centre of the pocket on the garment. A jet pocket can be any length, though not usually longer than 15cm (6in), and any width.

Cut two strips four times the finished width of one side, and fold in half. These are easier to attach if the turnings are the same width as the *beading*. The front pocket bag should be shorter by the width of the whole jet pocket.

There are 1-cm ($\frac{3}{8}$-in) turnings throughout this diagram.

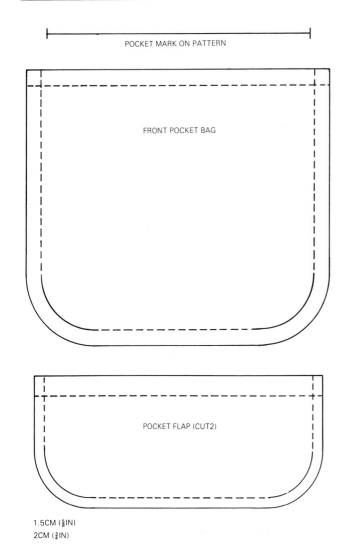

POCKET MARK ON PATTERN

FRONT POCKET BAG

POCKET FLAP (CUT2)

1.5CM ($\frac{5}{8}$IN)
2CM ($\frac{3}{4}$IN)

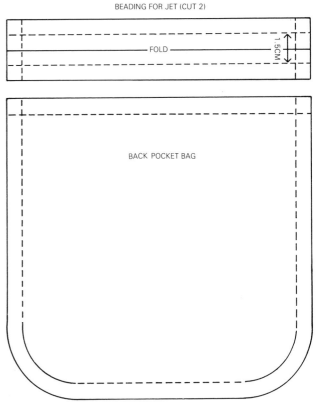

BEADING FOR JET (CUT 2)

FOLD

1.5CM

BACK POCKET BAG

Jet pocket with flap

Follow the directions for the jet pocket.

In this diagram the strips of beading are 0.75cm ($\frac{5}{16}$ in) wide, so all the turnings that are attached to them are the same width. The other turnings are 1cm ($\frac{3}{8}$in). The flap's top turning is 0.75cm ($\frac{5}{16}$ in), and the outer edge is 0.5cm ($\frac{1}{4}$in).

Natural and Synthetic Fabrics

Left-hand column, top to bottom:
Viyella (wool/cotton mix)
Wool crêpe
Crinkled polyester
Broderie Anglaise
Grosgrain
Mohair
Cotton drill
Linen

Second column, top to bottom:
Calico
Needlecord
Jap silk
Printed cotton
Wild silk
Canvas
Wool bouclé
Fine linen

Third column, top to bottom:
Taffeta
Muslin
Brushed acrylic
Silk velvet
Viscose
Heavy open-weave cotton
Wool flannel
Cotton gingham

Fourth column, top to bottom:
Acetate lining
Cotton jersey
Heavy wool
Corduroy
Fine wool
Herringbone silk
Crêpe de chine
Denim

Right-hand column, top to bottom:
Wool jersey
Polyester
Lightweight cotton
Moiré
Felt
Herringbone worsted
Seersucker
Piqué

Fabrics

The great variety of fabrics available today comes from surprisingly few raw materials – four main natural sources: wool, cotton, linen, and silk, and five main categories of synthetic: acetate, acrylic, nylon, polyester, and viscose.

The wide range of resulting fabrics is determined by different methods of spinning, weaving, and finishing, and by the blending and mixing of different fibres and yarns.

The list below gives brief descriptions of all the principal fabrics, with some practical comments on how to handle them. I always prefer to use natural fabrics but there are many people who are prepared to sacrifice the feel and quality of unblended cotton or linen, real silk and pure wool for the convenience of man-made fibres.

Acetate
A man-made, cellulose-based fibre that can be woven or knitted, and is frequently used for linings.

Acrylic
One of the principal man-made fibres, used mainly as a substitute for wool, or blended with it.

Alpaca
Light, soft and silky wool, from the alpaca llama. Sometimes blended with other wools, cotton, or man-made fibres.

Angora
Fine, soft rabbit-hair wool, strictly speaking from the angora rabbit only. Usually blended with other wools or man-made fibres.

Barathea
Fine, smooth, closely woven woollen fabric, traditionally black or dark blue. Should always be pressed with a damp cloth to avoid causing a shine on the surface.

Bouclé
Rich, textured woollen or wool-mix fabric woven from thick, slubby yarn. Needs careful handling to avoid snagging the threads.

Brocade
Heavy, rich fabric made on a jacquard loom, incorporating decorative patterns. Metallic threads are often included. Originally silk, but now more often synthetics.

Broderie Anglaise
Decorative fabric combining embroidery with small open areas. Used for whole garments or for edging. Usually cotton but can be fine wool or nylon.

Calico
Light, plain-weave cotton, sometimes printed with small decorative patterns. An ideal material for making toiles and practising shapes.

Canvas
General term for heavy, plain woven cotton, linen, or synthetics. Often used as interfacing in tailoring because of its natural stiffness.

Cashmere
Soft, luxury fibre from the cashmere goat, usually blended with other wool to reduce the cost and improve durability. Delicious worn next to the skin.

Challis
Light, soft, plain woven wool, often with printed paisley decoration. Hangs beautifully, but needs care during machining and pressing to avoid stretching.

Cheesecloth
Very loosely woven cotton fabric, usually from India. A favourite of the hippy generation.

Chenille
Fuzzy, caterpillar-like yarn, with a pile standing out at right angles. It can be woven or knitted, and is made of silk, wool or man-made fibres.

Chiffon
Smooth, lightweight woven fabric, in silk or in man-made equivalents. Difficult to machine; a layer of tissue paper can be used to stop it slipping.

Cire
A very shiny, slippery surface applied to a variety of fabrics at the finishing stage.

Corduroy
Velvety, corded fabric, with ribs of various widths from fine needlecord to chunky elephant cord. It should always be cut one way, as it has a *nap*. Usually made of cotton.

Cotton
One of the principal natural fibres, from many varieties of cotton plant. Strong, tough, and absorbent, it is the most versatile of fibres. Though synthetics can avoid cotton's tendency to crease, none can match its fresh tactile qualities.

Crêpe
Woven fabric with a crinkly surface, achieved by various weaving techniques such as the use of tightly twisted yarns. A lovely clinging fabric when cut on the bias. Tends to stretch, but can be shrunk back into shape.

Crêpe de Chine
Sheer, lightweight silk crêpe. Difficult to work with, but well worth the effort.

Cretonne
Heavyweight, plain-weave cotton or cotton-blended fabric. Used extensively for curtains and upholstery.

Damask
Decorative textured fabric, based on the combination of a variety of weave patterns. Made mostly in wool, cotton or silk.

Denim
Tough cotton or cotton-blend twill-weave fabric. Traditionally with blue warp and white filling yarns. The cult material of the 1960s and 1970s. One of the few fabrics believed to improve with age.

Drill
Tough, medium-weight twill-weave fabric, in cotton or cotton-blend fabrics.

Fake fur
A rich pile fabric, usually acrylic, providing a socially acceptable alternative to traditional fur.

Felt
A thick, non-woven woollen fabric, made by compression. Easily shaped for such items as hats, but too weak in tension to be suitable for whole garments.

Flannel
Medium-weight plain or twill woollen fabric, with a napped finish. Traditional colour associations of white flannels for sport, grey flannel suits, and red flannel petticoats.

Flannelette
A lightweight, usually cotton, version of flannel, commonly used for children's wear and warm sheets.

Fusible fabrics See p. 78-9.

Gaberdine
Firm, tightly woven twill fabric, originally woollen, but now in a variety of fibres. Tough and weather resistant, hence its association with rainwear.

Georgette
Sheer fabric similar to chiffon, but with the texture of crêpe. Hangs beautifully when cut on the bias.

Gingham
Plain-weave cotton or cotton blends with regular patterns, usually in the form of the familiar check. When cutting it is important to ensure that the checks match up.

Grosgrain
Heavy, ribbed fabric, woven with a crosswise effect. Often used for ribbons.

Harris tweed
Hand-woven tweed from woollen yarns from the Outer Hebrides. Strong and hardwearing, an ideal material for coats, suits and jackets.

Herringbone
Any twill-weave fabric with the distinctive chevron pattern.

Interfacing See p. 78–9.

Jap Silk
Lightweight, plain weave silk.

Jersey
Fine-gauge, machine-knitted fabric, designed to be cut and sewn.

Lamé
Fabric woven from, or including, metallic yarns.

Lawn
Sheer, lightweight, plain-weave fabric. Originally linen, now cotton or cotton blends. Often printed with small-scale floral decorations. A crisp, fresh-feeling fabric.

Leatherette
Vinyl-coated fabric supposed to imitate leather.

Linen
Fabric woven from flax fibres, now often unfortunately blended with synthetics to prevent creasing. Pure linen is deliciously cool in summer and warm in winter. Weights range from fine handkerchief linen to much heavier weaves.

Mohair
Wool from the Angora goat, woven to form a tough yet smooth and shiny fabric, popular for men's suitings.

Moiré
A decorative 'watery' effect applied to the surface of fabrics. Particularly good on silk, but also found on cottons and synthetics.

Muslin
Plain, lightweight cotton or cotton-blend fabrics.

Net
Open mesh fabric, used lavishly in 'Come Dancing' dresses, as well as for sleeves and veils.

Nylon
One of the principal man-made fibres, more correctly known as polyamide. Tough, strong, drip-dry and crease resistant, but lacking the breathing qualities and appeal of natural fibres.

Organdie and Organza
Lightweight but relatively stiff open-weave fabric, originally cotton (organdie) or silk (organza).

Piqué
Textured cotton or cotton-blend fabric, with decorative patterns raised on the surface.

Polyester
One of the most common man-made fibres, extremely versatile in its own forms, but a poor substitute for the natural fibres it imitates.

Poplin
Fine, tightly woven fabric with a crosswise rib. Originally a combination of silk and worsted. Popular for shirts and pyjamas.

Sailcloth
A form of firmly woven canvas, in cotton or man-made fibres.

Satin
A smooth, shiny weave, with a lustrous, unbroken surface. Advisable to press on the reverse side, which often has a crêpe or similar texture. Made in cotton, silk or polyester.

Seersucker
A textured cotton weave achieved by varying the yarn tensions. Once made up it should not require subsequent pressing.

Shantung
Silk, or now often synthetic, fabric including large, slub, or irregular yarns in one direction, to give a distinctive texture.

Silk
The traditional luxury fibre, spun from the silkworm's continuous thread. Woven into a wide variety of fabrics (see also Jap silk and wild silk). Unfortunately silk is increasingly replaced by man-made substitutes. Fine silk needs careful handling as it marks very easily, but it is lovely to wear.

Sweatshirt fabric
Jersey fabric with a soft pile reverse, in cotton or acrylic, but giving the warmth of wool.

Taffeta
A crisp, rustling, plain-weave fabric, traditionally silk but now, unfortunately, as likely to be synthetic.

Tweed
A range of rough, medium-weight woollen fabrics, usually including slubs or yarn or knots, on a hairy surface.

Velvet and Velour
Fabrics with short, smooth, closely woven pile. They should be cut one way, with the pile running smooth up, not down, the body. A special velvet board is desirable for pressing.

Viscose
The general title for the synthetic fibres that include rayon, one of the first man-made fabrics. Viscose fibres are designed to imitate a variety of natural fibres, and are often blended with them.

Viyelia
A proprietory but generally recognized name for a twill cloth similar to a fine flannel, consisting of 55 per cent wool and 45 per cent cotton.

Voile
Lightweight, sheer cotton fabric, woven from tightly twisted yarn. Ideal for blouses and lingerie.

Wet-look fabrics
Fabrics such as ciré or PVC, that have a shiny, unbroken surface.

Wild silk
A rough form of silk with a dull surface, from uncultivated silkworms.

Wool
Natural animal hair, usually from sheep, but sometimes goat, llama, and rabbit. Warm, resilient, and versatile, ranging from the smoothest barathea to the chunkiest tweed. Wool is frequently blended with man-made fibres, mainly to make it easier to wash.

Worsted
A specially tough and smooth woollen yarn.

Costings and Pattern Lays

When the pattern, with seam allowances, is completed, and the chosen fabric width is known, a costing can be worked out by trying out different arrangements of pattern pieces. The aim is to arrange them until they fit into the smallest possible area of fabric.

It is usually more economical to lay the pattern on unfolded fabric. The examples illustrated below show the same pattern laid on folded and unfolded fabric, with considerable savings on the latter.

In some cases an economical *lay* can save so much fabric at you can afford a better quality.

The right side of the fabric

It is important to identify the right side of the fabric before laying on the pattern. Often it is clear, but sometimes careful examination is needed to tell the right from the wrong side. One means of identification is the way the fabric is folded: cottons and linens are right side out; wools, wrong side out. If fabric is rolled into a tube the right side faces out.

When there is no visible difference between the sides, make one the back and mark it with chalk to avoid possible confusion.

One-way fabrics

Some fabrics, such as velvet, are clearly one-way, because they have a *nap*. In the case of velvet the nap should be laid so as to feel smooth up, not down, the body.

With other fabrics it is sometimes hard to tell whether or not they are one-way. An effective way of telling is to drape a length of the fabric around your own neck, and look down at the two sides to see if they shade in the same way. If there is a difference, then it is a one-way fabric, and the pattern must be laid on in one direction. If there is no perceptible difference the fabric can be used either way.

General points to remember

● If a fabric is folded when bought, make sure that the crease is removable.

● Some patterns will fit economically into only one particular width of fabric, and can be very costly when laid on other widths.

● The right side of the fabric should be inspected while you are arranging the pattern pieces, so that you can see if there are any flaws in the surface.

● The grain line on every pattern piece must be kept parallel to the selvedge. The grain line on a *bias cut* pattern piece must also lie parallel to the selvedge in order for the pattern to be on the true bias.

● When pattern pieces are laid on to the fabric they can be placed almost touching each other. There is no need to allow extra fabric as well as the seam allowances. Try to cut around the patterns exactly.

● When laying the pattern on to opened-out fabric mark the duplicate pieces in with chalk, making sure they are an exact pair.

● Some pattern pieces have RSU (right side up) marked on them because they are not a pair.

● Lay out all pattern pieces before starting to cut out.

● Checks and stripes should be matched wherever possible. Match them on the fitting line not on the outer edge.

● If some of the pattern pieces will not quite fit into a standard width of fabric, try changing the position of the side seams to re-spread the volume.

● Make sure all the information from the pattern has been transferred to the fabric before removing the pattern.

Sometimes in industry the quantity of fabric is decided before the garment has been designed. In that case the design has to be worked out to fit into the available fabric without any waste.

Pressing

Pressing is not the same as ironing. Pressing does not involve sliding the iron over the surface of the fabric, but simply pressing down, lifting, and moving to the next section.

When pressing, bear the following points in mind:
● Always press an odd scrap first, to determine the best technique for the fabric.
● Press on the wrong side of the fabric. If it is necessary to press on the right side use a pressing cloth to prevent shine.
● Press with the grain of the fabric, and be careful not to stretch the edges by pulling the fabric.
● Pressing wool requires a lot of steam. If no steam iron is available use a damp pressing cloth.
● Do not use *too much* steam or moisture, as this can cause water marks or puckering.
● Press the fabric to be used before starting to cut into it. Pre-shrink if necessary.
● Press during making up, for example before seams and darts are crossed with other seams.
● Press vertical darts towards the centre, and horizontal darts downwards.
● Have some strips of thick paper to hand to slide between pleats and the wrong side of the garment, to prevent ridges being pressed through to the right side.
● When iron-on interfacings are used, attach them as soon as the garment is cut out. Make sure that the adhesive side does not touch the iron. If adhesive does get on to the surface of the iron it can be removed with an iron cleaner, available from haberdashers. Remember also not to put interfacings on to the turnings.
● Wherever possible press instead of tacking, especially on difficult corners and pockets.
● Never press over pins, as they will leave an impression in the fabric.
● Do not press any sharp creases until the garment is right, as they are very hard to remove.
A variety of equipment is available to help achieve special effects and shapes. It can mostly be found in haberdashers, but the two specialist shops mentioned on p.10 will have all of it.

Pounding block (or clapper)
A block of wood used with steam to flatten seam edges. First apply as much steam as possible with a steam iron and a damp pressing cloth. Then remove iron and cloth and pound firmly along the required edge.

Needle board (or velvet board)
A bed of short, upright needles mounted on heavy canvas backing. When a pile fabric is placed pile side downwards on the board the needles prevent the pile from being flattened when pressed.

Tailor's ham
A firmly stuffed oblong cushion, with subtly rounded curves, to facilitate the pressing of curved areas of a garment, such as darts and sleeve heads. Hams come in different sizes, with one side cotton and one side wool.

Point presser
A shaped piece of wood, providing many different forms for pressing points, curves, and edges.

Press mitt
A padded, glove-like cushion to fit over the hand. It has pockets on either side, to protect the hand, and is used for pressing rounded sleeve heads and small, hard to reach areas. It can also be slipped over the end of the sleeve board.

Sleeve board
Some ironing boards have sleeve boards attached. If not, it is well worth buying one, to provide a narrow, flat surface on which to press sleeve seams, trouser seams, and neck edges.

Seam roll
A firmly stuffed, cylindrical cushion that is rounded at each end. It is used to press long, curved seams in very narrow areas.

Clothes brush
This should always be available when pressing, for raising the *nap* of the fabric after pressing, and for removing any shine caused by over-pressing.

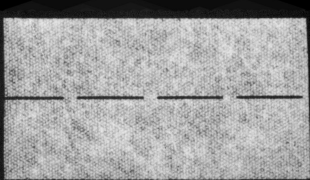

Interfacings

Choosing the correct interfacing is as important as matching the sewing threads or selecting the appropriate trimmings. When making your choice, handle the fabric and interfacing together to make sure that the feel is right. It may be necessary to use two different kinds of interfacing in the same garment, a heavier one for collars and lapels, and a lighter one for flaps, pockets, and other detailed areas.

Choose an interfacing with the same wash and/or dry-cleaning instructions as the fabric.

Before starting to make the garment test the interfacing by pressing or sewing a small piece to the fabric.

To apply iron-on interfacing place the adhesive side down on the wrong side of the fabric. Cover with a damp cloth and press hard with a hot, dry iron. Use a pressing action, not an ironing action, and leave to cool before handling. To apply sew-in interfacing is much more laborious and requires a small seam allowance (0.25cm [⅛in]) so that the interfacing can be tacked

Fold-a-band (firm) Iron-on

Used to stiffen waistbands. The centre slits provide a guide for pressing the centre fold, and the outside slits help to give a crisp edge for attaching the waistband to the garment.

Note: sometimes the turnings of the Fold-a-band can make the band too rigid, especially if the inside edge of the waistband is overlocked and left flat. In this case the turnings of the Fold-a-band should be cut off before starting (see p.102-3).

Fold-a-band (light) Iron-on

Specially designed for pleats, cuffs, pockets, and waistbands in lighter fabrics. Fold-a-band has slits along the centre line, which ensure that once a fold is ironed in it will hold permanently. It is

1   2   3   4   5

ideal for any part of a garment required to hold its pleat or fold throughout wear and tear.

Wundaweb Iron-on

For hems on dresses, skirts, and trousers. Wundaweb will work on most fabrics, but should be tested first on a small sample of the material to be used. Wundaweb is applied as follows:

- Fold the hem and press.
- Place Wundaweb inside the hem so that it is completely covered.
- Cover with a damp cloth.
- Press firmly with a hot, dry iron. Hold the pressure for ten seconds, or until the cloth is dry. Move along the hem and repeat.
- Allow to cool for ten minutes before handling.

Sew-in and iron-on interfacings

Sew-in interfacings are preferred by some, and are often used with fabrics such as velvet, corduroy, and seersucker. They are available in heavy weight (1), medium weight (2), and light weight in charcoal grey (3), and white (4).

Two special iron-on interfacings are available for use with cotton or cotton-blend fabrics, particularly for small detail areas which need a clean, crisp finish, such as collars and cuffs. These come in a firm weight (5), and a light weight (6).

Easy-fuse iron-on interfacings, such as Vilene's Ultrasoft, have been designed to give a soft, subtle handle to the fabric. The adhesive, applied in a series of dots, fuses at a relatively low temperature. Easy-fuse interfacings can be cut in any direction, giving maximum economy of use. They are available in heavy weight (7), medium weight (8), and light weight in charcoal grey (9) and white (10).

A super-stretch easy-fuse interfacing is also available (11), designed specially for use with stretch fabrics such as knits and jerseys. It too fuses at a low temperature, with a system of adhesive dots on the fusible side. It can be used on large or small areas, and will stretch and return with the fabric.

6   7   8   9   10   11

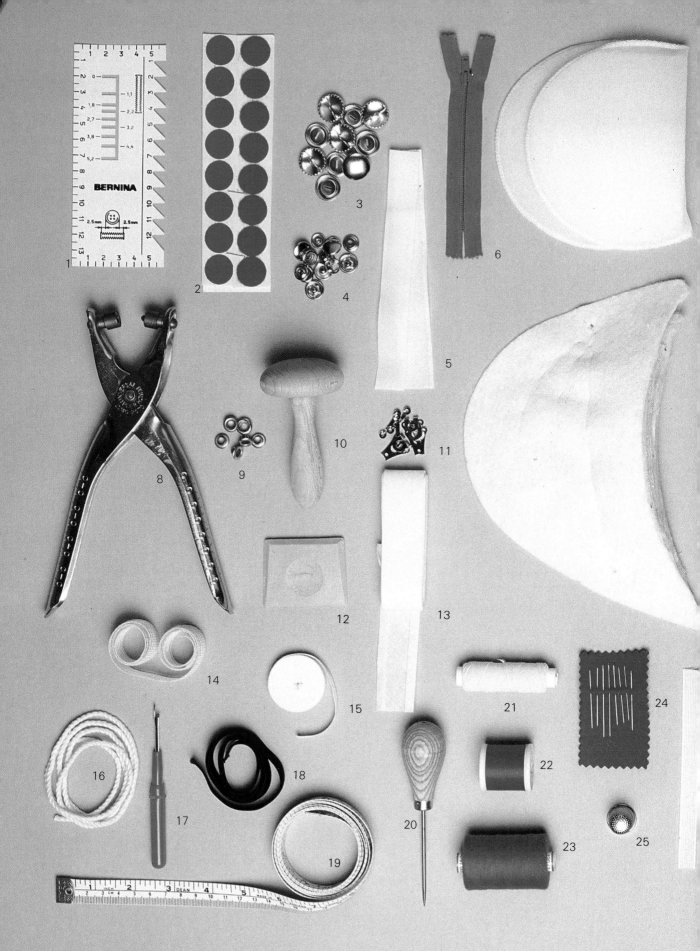

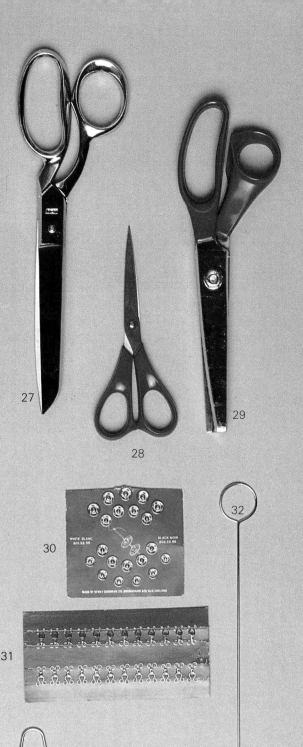

Haberdashery

1 Button gauge
Used for measuring the diameter and thickness of a button (see p. 85).

2 Velcro dots
These can be used in place of buttons, zips, or other fastenings.

3 Cover buttons
Usually covered with the same fabric as the garment.

4 No-sew snap fasteners
Clipped into the fabric.

5 Velcro strip
Another fastening system.

6 Zip fastener
The right weight must be selected, as well as the right length.

7 Shoulder pads
Two examples from the numerous types available.

8 and 9 Eyelet maker and eyelets
Available in various sizes and colours.

10 Darning toadstool
Used to support the area to be darned.

11 Trouser hooks
An alternative to buttons on the waistband.

12 Tailors' chalk
For transfering information from pattern to fabric, and for marking buttonholes.

13 Bias binding (wide)
Available in two widths, and in a range of colours.

14 Open-weave elastic
Used when elastic is to be stitched through to the garment.

15 Tape for seams
White or black woven tape 0.5cm ($\frac{1}{4}$in) wide, used to prevent seams from stretching (see p. 87), or for hanger loops.

16 Piping cord
For piping seams, available in many thicknesses.

17 Quick-unpic
For unpicking stitching, and slitting worked buttonholes.

18 Elastics
Available in different widths and strengths, usually black or white.

19 Tape measure
An essential item, worth having in a good enough quality to resist stretching.

20 Bradawl
A carpentry tool that is very useful when machining, for tucking under difficult corners.

21 Shirring elastic
Elasticated thread used in the bobbin of the machine to gather up the fabric automatically.

22 Sewing thread
This example is a cotton-covered polyester, which can be used on all fabrics.

23 Tacking cotton
100 per cent cotton used for *toiles* and tacking because it breaks easily.

24 Needles
'Sharps', sizes 1–12, are generally most useful.

25 Thimble

26 Whalebone
Plastic strip machined into strapless bodices for support.

27 Dressmaking shears
Available in different sizes and quality. Bent-handle shears are often preferred for cutting fabric.

28 Small, sharp-pointed scissors
Useful while machining, for clipping and trimming.

29 Pinking shears
Used for neatening edges, or for a decorative edge on non-woven fabrics.

30 Snap fasteners
Available in black, silver, or clear plastic, in various sizes.

31 Hooks and eyes
It is advisable to make a chainstitch loop in place of the metal eye, to hold the hook flatter and appear less obtrusive.

32 Rouleau hook
Used for turning the *rouleau* through.

33 Binding maker
Very useful if lots of bindings are needed. The bias cut fabric is threaded through to form binding.

34 Darning needle

35 Hair grips
An alternative *rouleau* hook.

36 Dressmaker's pins
Sharper, thinner, better quality pins are less liable to snag the fabric.

Forty Points to Remember when Making Up

The Sewing Machine
Make sure that:

1 The machine needle is sharp, and the right thickness and shape for the fabric:
— a sharp point needle for all types of woven fabric.
— a ball point needle for sewing knits.
— a wedge point needle for leather and vinyls.
2 The tension is right for the fabric.
3 The pressure is right for the fabric.
4 The correct sewing cotton is used.
5 The bobbin is full enough.
6 The stitch is a suitable length.

Seam Allowances
Make sure all seam allowances are clearly marked. Remember to use the right widths in the right places (see p.11).

Narrow Seam Allowances
Always use 0.5cm ($\frac{1}{4}$in) on all edges that are to be faced and *bagged out*, such as pockets, collars, cuffs, necklines, and sleeveless armholes.

Handsewing
There is little need for handsewing when making the sort of clothes described in this book. In industry almost everything is done by machine, and the same can apply at home. The only processes that should require hand sewing are hemming, sewing on buttons and hooks and neatening the back of bound buttonholes, sewing in shoulder pads, and catching down facings.

Tight Selvedges
Some selvedges are woven tight and tend to pull the fabric. Before cutting out the fabric clip the selvedge at intervals until it lies flat. Do not include a tight selvedge in the garment.

Tailor Tacking
No tailor tacking is necessary. Important points such as darts, pleats, pocket positions, and gathers can more easily be marked with tailor's chalk, a chalk pencil, or even an ordinary soft (2B) pencil. When marking pocket positions on the right side place the marks 0.5cm ($\frac{1}{4}$in) in, so that the pockets will cover them.

Press instead of Tacking
Press turnings under instead of tacking, to save time.

Clipping
If the right width seam allowances are used there will be *no need for clipping seams,* with the exception of seams that have 1.5-cm ($\frac{5}{8}$-in) turnings and are curved, such as a bust seam. Here the convex curve should be clipped, and the concave curve should have wedges cut out of the seam allowances. Stagger the clips and the wedges so as not to weaken the seam.

Layering
It is not usually necessary to layer turnings if the right seam allowances are added. But if the fabric is very thick, or if there are more than two layers in the seam, then it is advisable to cut them to different widths to reduce the bulk.

Reverse Machining
At the beginning and at the end of a row of machining there is no need to tie the ends of the thread together to stop the stitching undoing. Instead, machine four stitches in reverse. But in the case of topstitching these reverse stitches can sometimes show, so the threads should be pulled through to the wrong side and sewn in.

Cutting Off Cottons
In the long run it saves a lot of time if you cut off sewing threads as soon as the seam has been sewn. Keep some small, sharp scissors next to the machine.

Parallel Pinning
When an important point is obscured by fabric during machining, for instance when making a jet pocket, mark the point with a pin placed in a parallel position, a little way to the left of the work. Alternatively a chalk line may be drawn horizontal to the sewing point.

Guide Lines
If there are no seam width measurements marked on the needle plate of your machine, draw three clear lines on to a strip of paper the width of the seam allowances from the needle, and tape it to the needle plate as a guide when sewing.

When machining watch the guide line and not the needle.

A Band of Pins on the Machine
Attach a strip of cotton fabric 3cm ($1\frac{1}{4}$in) wide around the shaft arm of the machine, for sticking pins into as they are removed from the machining, and vice versa.

Pins and Machining
It is important to remove pins as you come to them, and not stitch over them and risk damaging the machine. Place the pins so that they point towards the machining, and can easily be pulled out before they are reached.

Bradawl
Keep a bradawl by the machine. It is an invaluable piece of equipment for tucking under difficult corners while machining.

Topstitching
1 Check that the bobbin is sufficiently full before starting topstitching.
2 Always start a row of topstitching in the least conspicuous place possible.
3 One row of topstitching next to a seam (which is in effect the same as *bluffing,* p.88) is often used on garments for decoration, to strengthen the seam, or to save pressing.
4 Hems and the ends of sleeves can often be finished off with two rows of topstitching. The edge is neatened and pressed up

(1.5cm[⅝in]). The first row is on the edge, and the second row is 1cm (⅜in) in from the edge.

This system is used especially on jersey fabrics and casual cotton and polyester/cotton garments.

5 Two rows of topstitching are often used on pockets, collars, yokes, cuffs, and belts, to give a more professional look. In these cases it is essential to keep the stitching straight.

Matching Seams

Make sure that all seams to be sewn together have matching balance notches, and are exactly the same length unless one is being eased into the other.

Bias Seams

Pull crossway/bias seams while they are being machined, to prevent the stitches snapping during wear.

Machining a Long Seam

When machining a long seam place the two pieces of fabric under the pressure foot at the beginning of the seam. Before machining pin the balance notches together along the seam, and the two ends together. *Do not* let the two pieces end up different lengths, as the finished shape will be distorted.

Machining from the Centre

When machining collars it is safer to machine from the centre back to the left-hand front, and then again from the centre back to the right-hand front. This ensures that the collar is centred, and makes it easier to stitch on.

Collar Points

When *bagging out* a collar which has points, such as shirt and rever collars, machine one straight stitch across the point, or two or three straight stitches on thicker fabrics. This will allow extra room for the turnings when the collar is turned through. All corners should be trimmed and tapered to reduce bulk, and the turnings should not overlap when the collar is turned through.

Collars and Cuffs

If collars or cuffs are being topstitched to a garment on the right side, press the turning to be topstitched under before starting to make up the piece.

Cuffs and Facings

Sew in-the-round when adding a cuff or facing to the end of a sleeve. Do not sew the cuff or facing on first and then sew up the sleeve seam, except when there is an opening in the sleeve seam instead of a placket. In this case the cuff is attached first.

Crotch Seam

The crotch seam of trousers or culottes should always be sewn together *after* sewing the inside leg seams. This helps them hang together properly. It is advisable to machine two identical rows along the crotch seam to strengthen it.

Taped Seams

Tape is sometimes added to a seam to keep it from stretching, or to strengthen it, in areas such as shoulder seams, waist seams, or necklines.

Side Seams on Dresses and Shirts

Try to attach pockets and sew in zips, collars, and yokes *before* sewing up the side seams. It is always easier to work when the fabric is flat.

Stay Stitching

Always stay stitch corners before clipping into them, in order to strengthen the weak point (see p. 110).

Shirt Sleeve Seam

When sewing the sleeve seam and underarm seam all in one, start from the underarm point and sew outwards. Do not sew over the underarm turning as this will cause the sleeve to pull from this point.

Stopping Elastic from Twisting

To stop the elastic in a waistband from twisting, machine a vertical line through it and both layers of fabric, at the centre front, centre back, and side seams.

Buttonholes

Buttonholes should extend 0.25cm (⅛in) on to the wrap, in order for the button to lie on the centre front line when done up.

Before cutting a worked buttonhole place a pin at right angles to it, inside the *bar tack*, to prevent cutting too far.

Hems

Hand sew between the hem and the garment, rather than over the edge, which would leave a line when the hem were pressed.

Gathering or Gauging

Use two rows of machining 0.25cm (⅛in) apart when gathering or gauging. When these threads are pulled up a ridge will appear between the rows. Attach the flat fabric by machining along the centre of the ridge, which should be the fitting line. Pull out the lower machining row which will be showing on the right side. This will give very even gathers.

Note: this should not be done on fine fabrics such as silks and polyesters, as the needle holes will remain visible. If in doubt test a piece to see (see p. 105).

Holding Row

Sometimes when a waistband, collar, or cuff is to be topstitched on to a garment the edge may have stretched and it will be hard to ease on neatly. A 'holding row' can be used to shrink this edge.

Place a finger immediately behind the foot of the machine and, while machining an ordinary row of stitching on to the stretched seam allowance, try to slow down the fabric moving through. This will cause a very slight gathering effect, which will shorten the length of the edge.

When the piece has been topstitched on to the garment it should be completely flat again, and the holding row will not be visible.

Shortening a Zip

A zip can be shortened quite simply by cutting it to the required length from the bottom, and over-sewing the last four teeth firmly together.

Buttons and Buttonholes

The buttonhole must be made exactly the right length to enable the button to pass through easily, and at the same time to hold the button securely in place.

The buttonhole size will depend on the thickness of the fabric and the size and depth of the button. As a general rule allow the button diameter plus 0.25cm ($\frac{1}{8}$in) for a flat button, and the button diameter plus 0.5cm ($\frac{1}{4}$in) for a thick button.

With thick fabrics the button requires a shank, to allow for the thickness of the material. Some buttons are made with a shank attached; otherwise a shank can be made with the cotton attaching the button to the cloth.

There are three kinds of buttonhole:

A bound buttonhole

This is made in exactly the same way as a jet pocket, but without the pocket bag being attached (see p.112). The facing behind the buttonhole is slit through, and cut into the corners. These edges are tucked under and sewn down by hand.

A machine-worked buttonhole

There are special attachments for sewing buttonholes, but any machine that has a zig-zag stitch can be used.

A hand-worked buttonhole

These are used mostly on tailored garments, to give a feeling of quality, or if no other means are available.

Points to remember

1 Buttonholes are placed on the right-hand side of a woman's garment, and on the left-hand side of a man's garment.

2 Space the buttonholes evenly. The top buttonhole, if not on a collar band, should be placed halfway between the neckline and the edge of the wrap.

3 Place a buttonhole at a point of tension, such as the bustline.

4 Never place a buttonhole on or near to the hem.

5 Always start with the bottom buttonhole, as they are likely to improve as you go along.

6 When working on a fine fabric or a jersey it is often helpful to machine the buttonhole through a piece of paper placed underneath, to stop the fabric puckering up. The paper can then be removed.

7 When a worked buttonhole is being machined on to a waistband, collar band, or cuff, the seam allowances can get in the way, and prevent the foot of the machine from lying flat. Place a strip of folded fabric under the foot, on the opposite side, to balance it.

8 On a trouser waistband the use of two small buttons instead of one larger one will help keep the band neatly secured.

The button wrap

The width of the wrap will be half the button's diameter plus 0.75cm ($\frac{5}{16}$ in), extended from the centre line. The button size must therefore be determined before the wrap is added to the pattern.

Buttons are sized in 'lignes', as follows:

18 ligne-1cm ($\frac{3}{8}$in)	36 ligne-2.2cm ($\frac{7}{8}$in)	60 ligne-3.8cm ($1\frac{1}{2}$in)
22 ligne-1.25cm ($\frac{1}{2}$in)	40 ligne-2.5cm (1in)	70 ligne-4.5cm ($1\frac{3}{4}$in)
26 ligne-1.5cm ($\frac{5}{8}$in)	45 ligne-2.75cm ($1\frac{1}{8}$in)	80 ligne-5cm (2in)
30 ligne-1.75cm ($\frac{3}{4}$in)	50 ligne-3.2cm ($1\frac{1}{4}$in)	

Positioning buttonholes

The centre front or back lines must be marked on each half of the garment, before the buttonholes are positioned.

● Horizontal buttonholes: the usual arrangement, extending 0.25cm ($\frac{1}{8}$in) beyond the centre line on to the wrap.

● Vertical buttonholes: often used on a *placket* front or when very small buttons are required, and placed directly on the centre line.

Positioning buttons

After making buttonholes place the centre lines of the two pieces on top of each other. For horizontal positions push a pin through the buttonhole, 0.25cm ($\frac{1}{8}$in) from the end nearest the finished garment edge, into the fabric beneath.

For vertical buttonholes the button should be positioned 0.25cm ($\frac{1}{8}$in) below the top of the buttonhole. The pin will mark the exact position of the button, on the centre line.

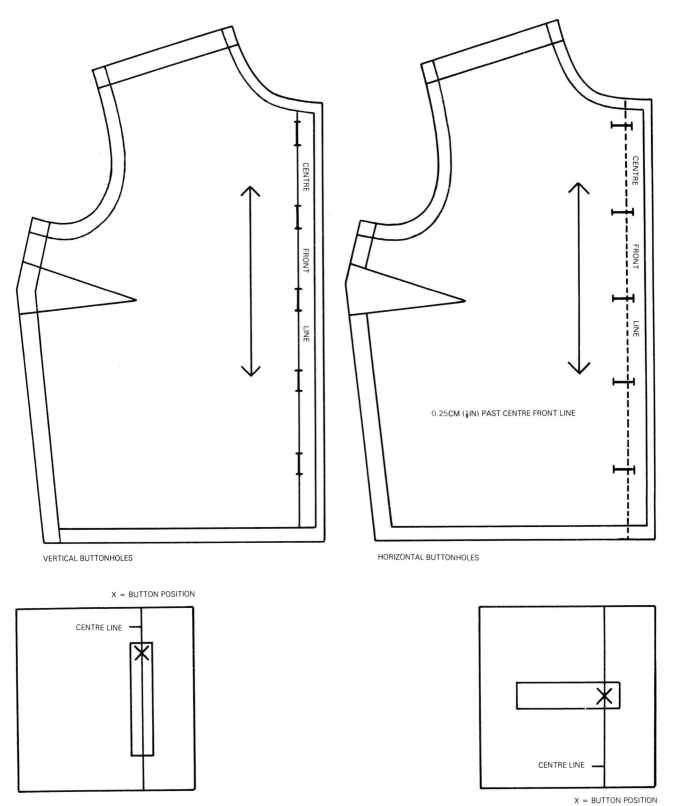

VERTICAL BUTTONHOLES

HORIZONTAL BUTTONHOLES

0.25CM (⅛IN) PAST CENTRE FRONT LINE

X = BUTTON POSITION

CENTRE LINE

CENTRE LINE

X = BUTTON POSITION

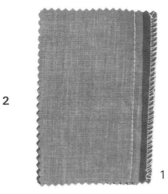

Quicker Ways of Making Up

This section shows in stages the way to put together important parts of a garment. In the black-and-white photographs the darker side of the fabric is the right side, and the paler side the wrong side.

Seams

1 French seam

(1.5cm [$\frac{5}{8}$in] seam allowance)
Fig.1 Lay wrong sides together and machine 0.5cm ($\frac{1}{4}$in) from edge. Press seam open.
Fig.2 Fold right sides together, press stitching line on edge, and sew along the fitting line so that the turnings are enclosed inside. Press seam to one side.

2 Welt seam

(1.5cm [$\frac{5}{8}$in] seam allowance. Trim top piece to 0.5cm [$\frac{1}{4}$in])
Fig.1 Place the two pieces right sides together and sew along fitting line.
Fig.2 Press top piece over and stitch 1cm ($\frac{3}{8}$in) from seam on the right side through the overlocked turning, trapping the small turning inside.

3 Flat felled seam

(2cm [$\frac{3}{4}$in] or 1.5cm [$\frac{5}{8}$in] seam allowance. Trim top piece to 0.5cm [$\frac{1}{4}$in])
Fig.1 Place the two pieces wrong sides together and sew along fitting line.
Fig.2 Press out flat and press turning under 0.5cm ($\frac{1}{4}$in).
Fig.3 Press the seam over to the left and topstitch it down.

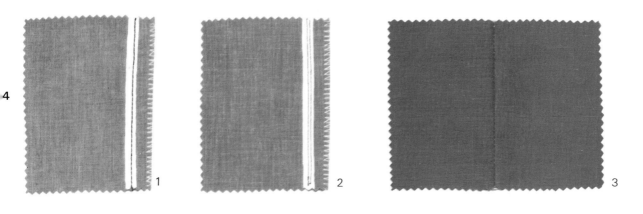

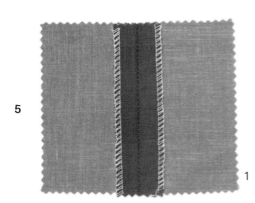

4 Taped seam

(1.5cm [⅝in] seam allowance)

Fig. 1 Attach tape to wrong side of fabric on one layer. The stitching line must be just inside the fitting line.

Fig. 2 Join the two pieces together along the fitting line.

Fig. 3 Press seam open.

5 Double topstitched seam

(1.5cm [⅝in] seam allowance)

Fig. 1 Make an ordinary open seam, overlock, and press open.

Fig. 2 Topstitch a row on either side of the seam.

6 Slot seam

(1.5cm [⅝in] seam allowance)

Fig. 1 Press seam allowances under and overlock. Overlock a strip 5cm (2in) wide.

Fig. 2 Lay the strip under the two edges and topstitch through. A gap can be left if a contrast fabric is being used, but take into account that this will make the garment a little larger.

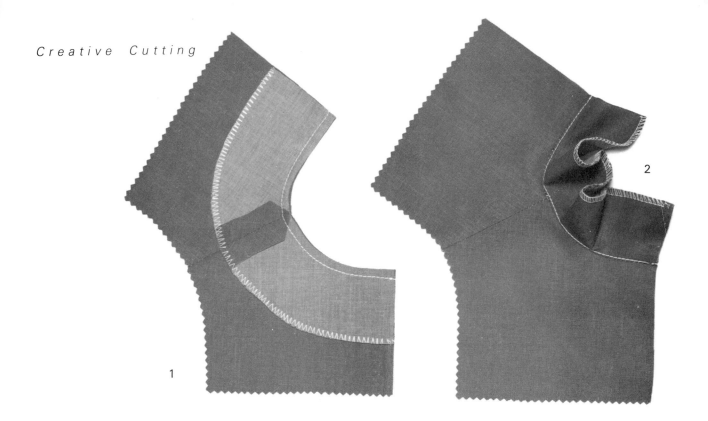

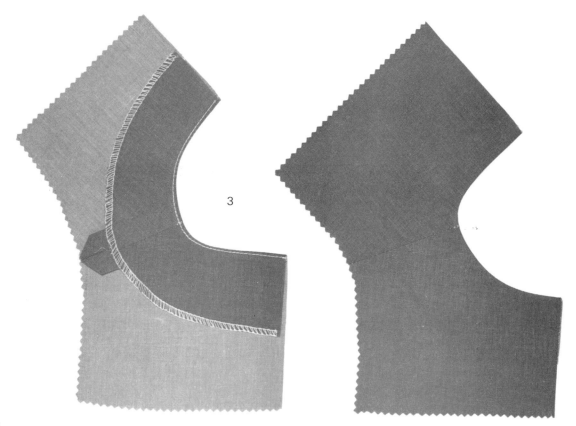

Facings

Fig. 1   Sew together shoulder seams of facing and garment.
Put right sides together and join neckline.

Fig. 2   Lift facing up and machine a row of *bluffing* (or under
stitching) through the three layers close to the edge. This will
help the facing to roll neatly to the wrong side (Fig. 3).

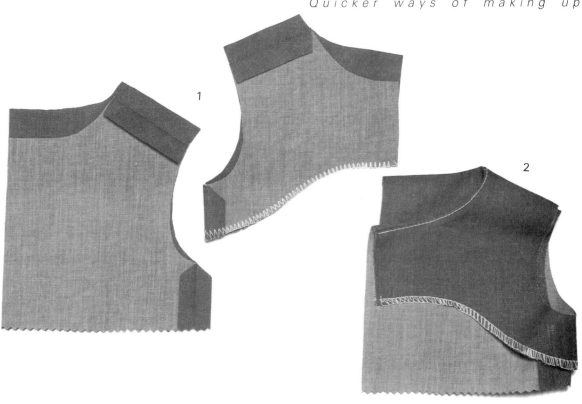

Bagging out neck and armholes in one

Fig. 1 Sew together back and front shoulder and side seams on facing and garment.

Fig. 2 Place right sides together and join neckline. *Bluff* neck edge.

Fig. 3 Work from the inside of the garment: at one armhole fold the front facing back, and make the armhole ends of the shoulder seams of the garment and facing meet, right sides together. The other half of the back bodice is between the front bodice and the front facing.

Stitch the front armhole of the garment and facing together from the shoulder seam to the underarm seam. Remove the work from the machine and fold the front facing back on to the front of the garment, wrong sides together.

Work exactly the same way for the back armhole, and overlap the stitching at the shoulder and underarm seam.

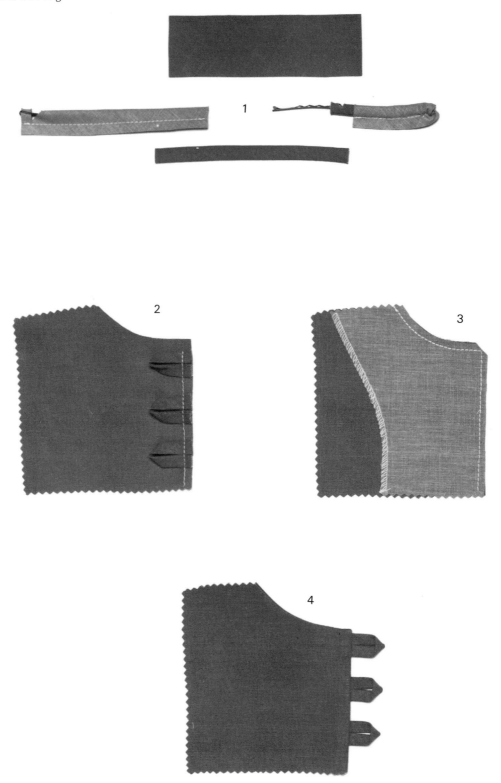

Rouleaux and rouleaux loops

Fig.1 *Rouleaux* are always cut on the true bias, machined on the wrong side, and turned through with the help of a hair grip or special rouleaux hook.

Fig.2 Attach *rouleaux* loops at regular intervals, with the seam on the inside of the loop. Make sure they are all the same length.

Fig.3 Machine the facing over them, covering the first row of stitching.

Fig.4 Turn facing to wrong side and press. Make sure the buttons will fit through the loops. The buttons will lie on the centre line.

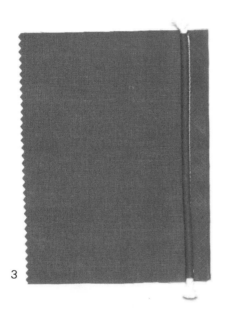

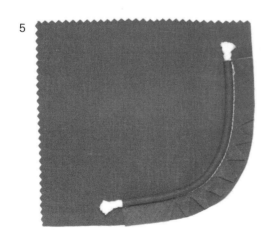

Piping

Fig.1 Join bias strips for piping on a straight grain.

Fig.2 Machine piping cord into a *rouleau*, using a zipper foot.

Fig.3 The turnings on the piping should be the same width as the turnings on the garment. Machine along the fitting line, using the zipper foot. Make sure that this row of stitching is on the piping side of the first row.

Fig.4 To attach the other piece of fabric, stitch along the fitting line, still using the zipper foot, as near as possible to the piping.

Fig.5 When piping on a curved edge, clip wedges out to make the piping lie flat on the curve. Otherwise follow instructions as for straight piping.

Fig.6 When piping at a corner, clip the corner to get a clean angle. Otherwise follow instructions as for straight piping.

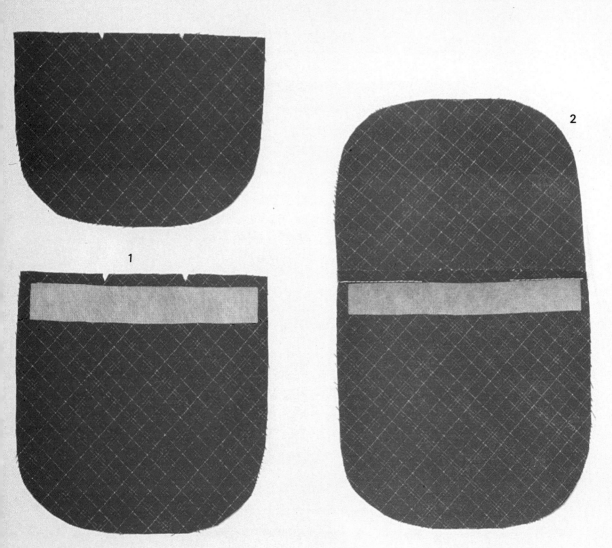

Bagging out (1)

Fig.1 Interface top edge of pocket.
Fig.2 Sew pocket pieces together, from outside edges to notch.
Fig.3 Fold along top of interfacing and sew the outer edges together with 0.5-cm (¼-in) turnings.
Fig.4 Turn pocket to right side through the hole left in the first seam. Press, and topstitch to garment.

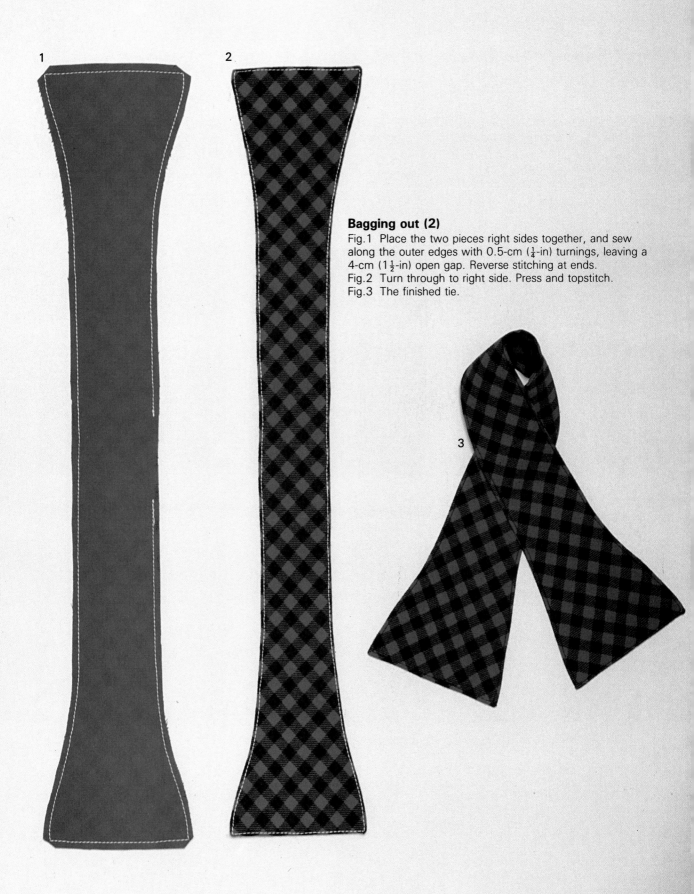

Bagging out (2)
Fig.1 Place the two pieces right sides together, and sew along the outer edges with 0.5-cm ($\frac{1}{4}$-in) turnings, leaving a 4-cm (1$\frac{1}{2}$-in) open gap. Reverse stitching at ends.
Fig.2 Turn through to right side. Press and topstitch.
Fig.3 The finished tie.

Bindings

Bindings are cut on the true bias, and joined together on the straight grain (Fig.4).

Fig.1 Sew binding on to the wrong side, with the turning pressed under. Bind the edge and topstitch on the right side.

Fig.2 Sew binding on to right side, bind edge, and sink stitch overlocked edge down from the right side.

Fig.3 Sew binding on to the right side, with the turning pressed under. Bind edge and sink stitch from the right side,

catching down the folded edge.

Fig.5 Using a double binding stitch to the right side, bind edge and sink stitch from the right side, catching down the double edge.

Fig.6 Using a double binding on a curved edge, stitch to the right side. Machine a row of topstitching along the folded edge. Bind the edge and sink stitch down from the right side, using this line as a guideline for the fingers.

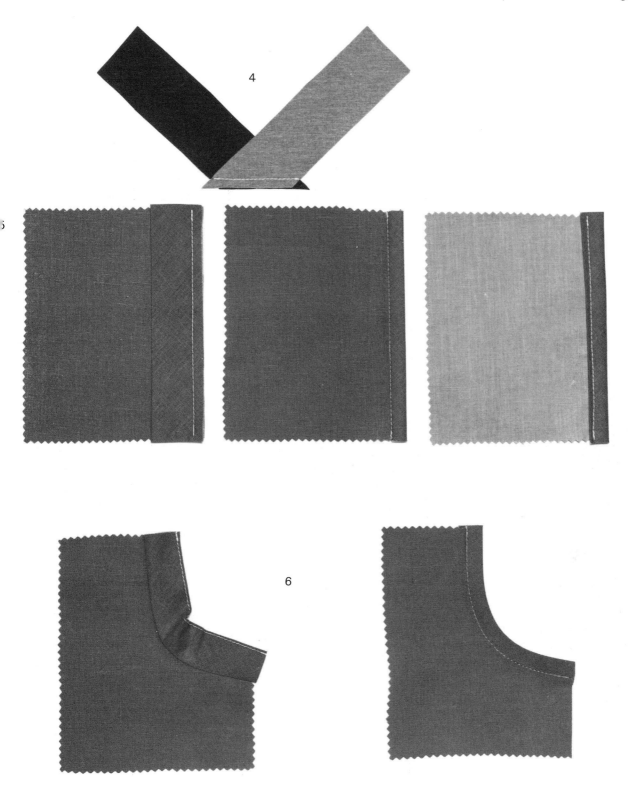

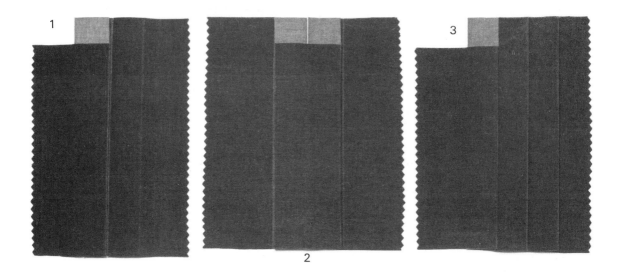

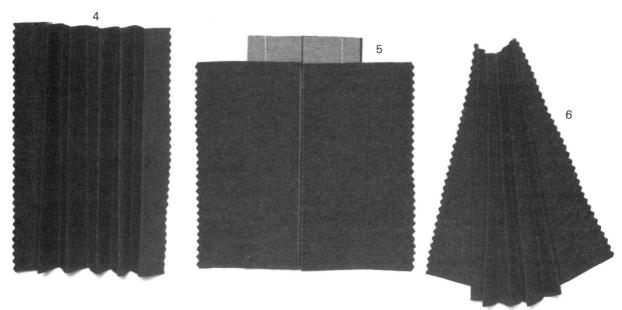

Pleats

Inverted pleat (Fig.1)
The same as two knife pleats facing each other, or the reverse of a box pleat.

Box pleat (Fig.2)
The reverse of an inverted pleat.

Knife pleats (Fig.3)
Single pleats running in the same direction (unless an inverted or box pleat is introduced to change the direction).

Accordion pleats (Fig.4)
Regular or graduated pleats, of any size. A pleating machine is required to form them.

Pleat with separate underlay (Fig.5)
An inverted pleat in appearance, but made with a separate underlay to form the underside. A contrasting colour can be used for the underlay.

Sunray pleats (Fig.6)
Radiating from a central point, and often used on half-circular skirts. A pleating machine is required to form them.

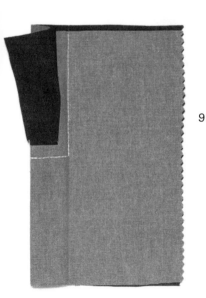

Seams in pleating (Fig.7)
When there is a seam in pleating, it can easily be concealed by being placed in a back fold of a pleat.

Topstitched inverted pleat (Fig.8)
To achieve this, sew down the pleat on the fold line to where the topstitching will end. Press in the pleat and flatten this seam. Cut down bulky turnings most of the way behind the seam, leaving enough for the topstitching to hold them in place. Topstitch through these turnings.

Self-stay stitched down inverted pleat (Fig.9A)
After stitching down the pleat stitch across both sides to the under fold. Slit the fold above the seam line. Trim away the under half to 1cm ($\frac{3}{8}$in) from the stitching.
(Fig.9B) Press the pleat and place the overlocked flap into its original position. Catch in the waistband.

Graduated pleats (Fig.10)
Tapered knife pleats, enabling a skirt to fit at the waist and on the hips. A pleating machine is required to form them.

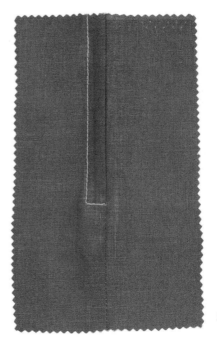

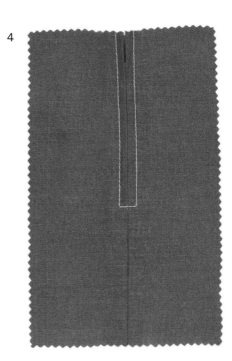

Zips

Zips should always be worked from the bottom to the top, to ensure that the positioning is right.

Lapped zip (Fig.1)
This is most often used at the left side seam of trousers, skirts, or dresses. Sew up seam to zip end, press, and stitch in right hand side of zip near the edge, starting from just below the end of the zip and inside seam.
Fig.2 Do up zip, and sew securely across the end and up the side of the zip. 1.25cm ($\frac{1}{2}$in) away from the edge.

Centred zip (Fig.3)
This is used at centre front or back of garments, or at edges of sleeves. Sew up seam to zip end, press, and stitch from centre of zip two stitches out to the right, and then up parallel to the edge.
Fig.4 Return to zip end and machine two stitches out to the left, and then up parallel to the edge. Pull threads at the lower point through to wrong side and secure.

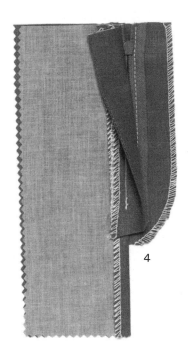

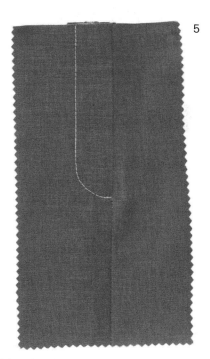

Trouser zip

This is used in the centre front of men's, and sometimes women's, trousers. In women's trousers it laps right over left.

Fig.1 First bag out the fly shield and press. Sew the crotch seam 4cm (1½in) to zip end. Press the turnings of the zip opening under, and topstitch the fly shield and zip to the left side of the garment, starting from just inside the crotch seam.

Fig.2 Attach the fly facing to the right front, along the fitting line, with right sides together.

Fig.3 Lay the fronts in position for the next stage, and hold right front down with pins.

Fig.4 Turn the garment to the wrong side, with the pins still in place, and stitch the tape of the zip to the fly facing. Pinning will help keep this line of stitching in the right place.

Fig.5 Turn to the right side and machine the final row, from the bottom of the zip (backwards and forwards at this point for extra strength) to the top, making a curved corner. Do not catch the fly shield in this row of stitching.

Continuous strip opening

Fig.1 Cut a strip 1cm (⅜in) longer than twice the length of the slit, and 1cm (⅜in) wider than twice the width.

Fig.2 Attach strip to slit.

Note: the turnings on the slit go off to nothing at the halfway mark.

Fig.3 Fold strip over to right side and topstitch down.

Fig.4 Press the strip that will end up on top inwards, and the other one outwards. The top of the folded strip can be stitched through to hold it in place.

Fig.3 *Bag out* the top section and trim the corner.
Clip in at the point where the two machine lines meet, at the top of the slit. Pass the placket through to the right side.
Fig.4 Turn the placket right side out, press edge of placket under, and topstitch in place.

Sleeve placket

Fig.1 Interface half of placket strip and slit the opening.
Fig.2 Turn under twice and stitch down the back edge of the placket. Attach the strip to the front edge on the wrong side.

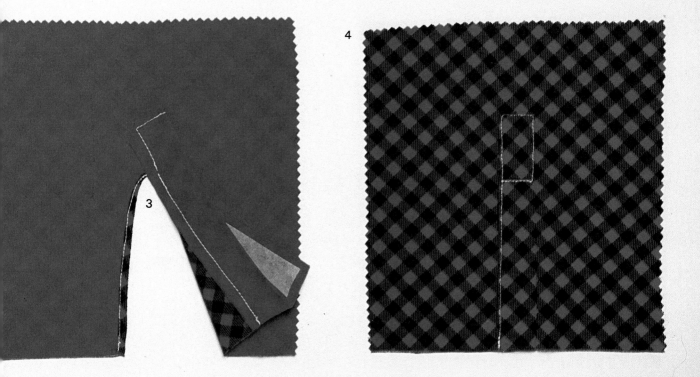

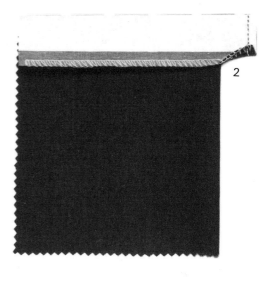

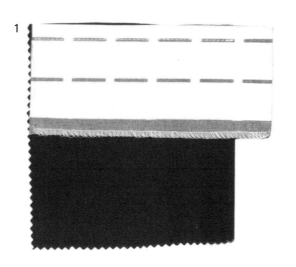

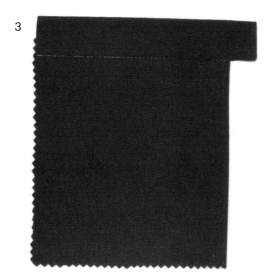

Waistbands

Fig.1 Iron on fold-a-band (firm) to the waistband, having cut off the interfacing turning on the overlocked edge. Sew the band on with right sides together from the edge with the seam allowances turned under (this is where the zip would be).

Fig.2 Fold band along top fold line and sew ends, catching in both turnings of the band. Trim corner.

Fig.3 Turn band through to right side out and press. Sink stitch from right side.

Fig.4 Catch the sink stitching in the overlocked turning, on the wrong side. The lower seam on the projection can be left unstitched, or hand slip stitched. When the skirt is done

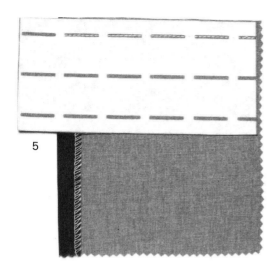

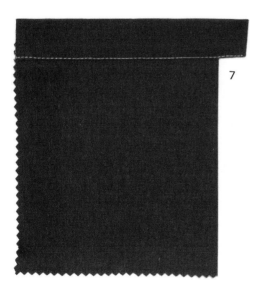

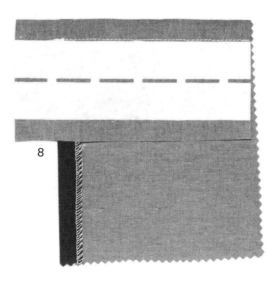

up it will be hidden, as the button is sewn on to this projection and not the buttonhole.

Fig.5 Iron on fold-a-band firm to the waistband. Sew the band with its right side to the wrong side of the garment, having pressed the turning of the garment to the wrong side.

Fig.6 Fold band along top fold line and sew end, catching in both turnings of the band. Clip corner.

Fig.7 Turn band through to right side out. Fold under turning and topstitch on to the right side.

Fig.8 This shows the same process as fig.5, but with no interfacing on seam allowances. This reduces the bulk, and is desirable with thicker fabrics. Proceed as from fig.5.

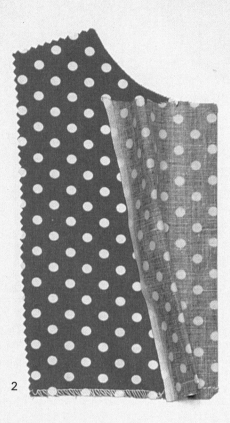

Fly front opening

Fig.1 Press along the fold lines.
Fig.2 Bag out the two ends separately at the hem. Trim corners and turn through to right side.
Fig.3 Stitch fly front in place, from right side.
Fig.4 Work buttonholes on under flap, before attaching collar.

Gathering

Fig.1 Sew two rows with a large stitch.
Fig.2 Draw up to the required length, and secure ends.
Fig.3 When using a silk or equivalent synthetic fabric, machine the gathering to the garment just below the stitching. With other fabrics, machine the gathering to the garment between the two rows of stitching, then pull out the lower row.
Fig.4 Two rows are used for easing, as with a sleeve head.

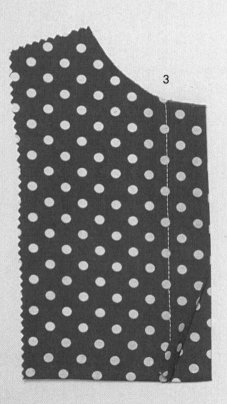

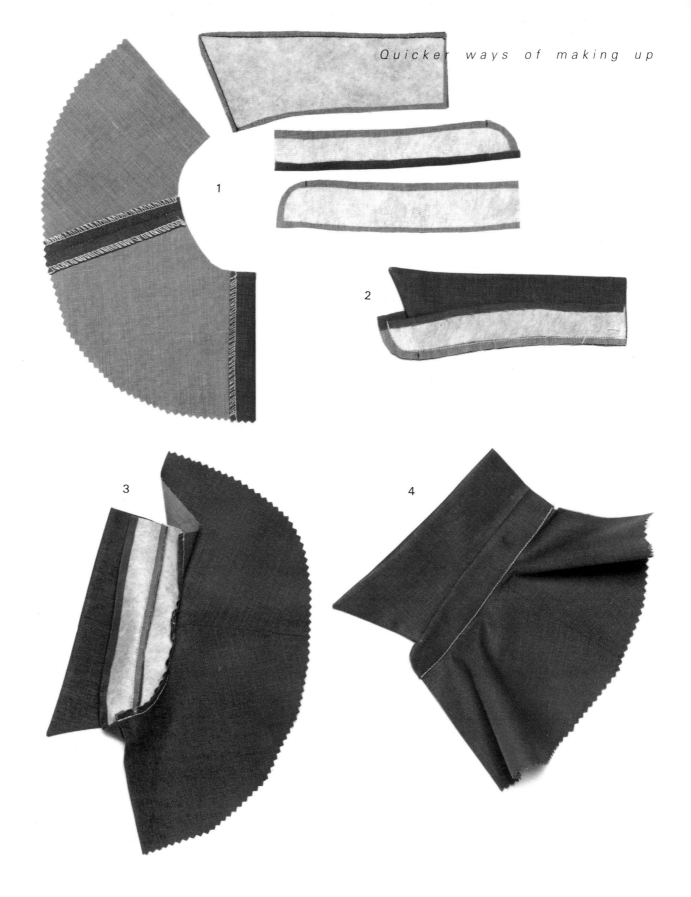

The shirt collar

Fig.1 Interface under collar and both collar stands. *Bag out* collar (with a straight stitch across the point). Trim corners, turn to the right side, and press. Topstitch if required. Sew shoulder seams and finish off front edge.
Fig.2 Sandwich collar between collar stands, and machine together.
Fig.3 Sew inside collar stand to neck edge.
Fig.4 Topstitch outside collar stand to neck edge. Press.

Cowl collar
Fig.1 Attach facing to back neck, and *bluff*.
Fig.2 Machine ends of folds, and sew cowl to front bodice.
Fig.3 Sew shoulder seams, and continue along facing seam.
Press seam open.
Fig.4 Press facings under, and catch them down at
shoulder. (Only half the cowl is shown
  in the photograph.)

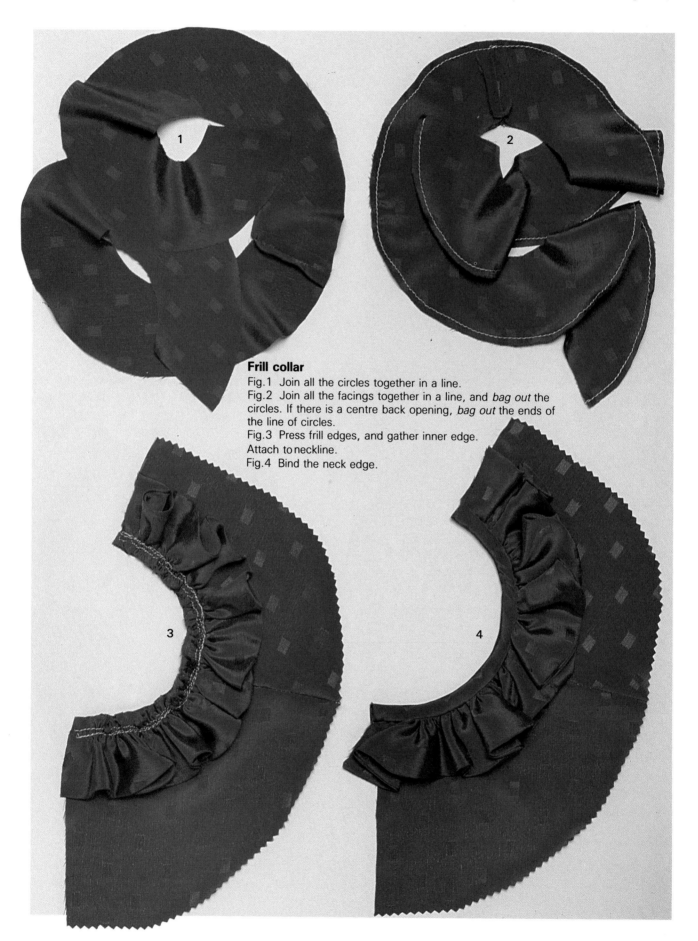

Frill collar

Fig.1 Join all the circles together in a line.

Fig.2 Join all the facings together in a line, and *bag out* the circles. If there is a centre back opening, *bag out* the ends of the line of circles.

Fig.3 Press frill edges, and gather inner edge. Attach to neckline.

Fig.4 Bind the neck edge.

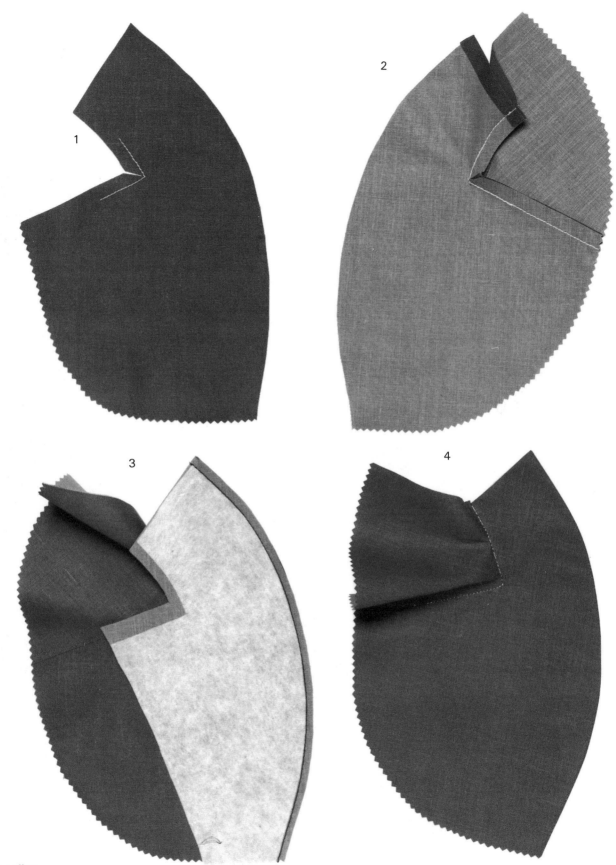

Shawl collar

Fig.1 Stay stitch neck point on front, and clip.

Fig.2 Join centre back, under collar seam. Press open.
Sew shoulder seams and back neck edge.

Fig.3 Interface top collar and front facing all in one. Sew
with right sides together, along outer edge.

Fig.4 Turn collar through, press, and overlock.
Sink stitch along back neckline and shoulder seams,
catching in the top collar and facings.
Clip into neck point. Gently press in roll line.
If desired the collar can be topstitched.

Peter Pan collar

Fig.1 Interface top collar and *bag out* (with a straight stitch across the point).

Fig.2 Turn collar to right side, press, and topstitch. Attach to neck edge.

Fig.3 Sew facing to front and neck edges, right sides together. Trim corners.

Fig.4 Turn facing over to wrong side and press. Topstitch up the front edge and follow round neck edge under collar. This is done through all the layers, to make a neat, flat edge, rather like *bluffing*.

Jet pocket, and jet pocket with flap

Fig.1 Cut two strips for the jet, four times the finished width, and 3cm (1¼in) longer than the finished pocket. Fold the strips in half. Mark the pocket position on the garment. Interface around this mark on the wrong side.

Fig.2 Sew the strips on to the right side, on either side of the pocket mark, with folded edges outwards.

Fig.3 Attach the pocket bag, by machining over the first rows of stitching.

Fig.4 Turn to wrong side and cut pocket hole along the

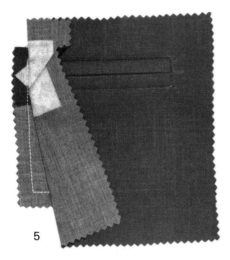

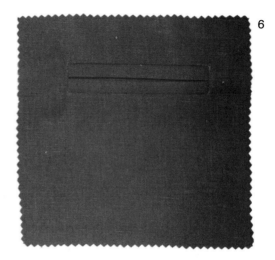

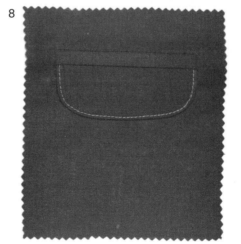

centre, and clip into the corners. Pull pocket through to wrong side and press.
Fig.5 Turn back to right side and lift up the sides. Sew down the V to the pocket bag, and continue round the bag and through the other V.

Fig.6 The completed jet pocket.
Fig.7 To make a jet pocket with a flap, interface the flap on both sides and *bag out*. Turn through and press. Topstitch.
Fig.8 Slide finished flap into pocket, and sink stitch into position through top seam of pocket strip.

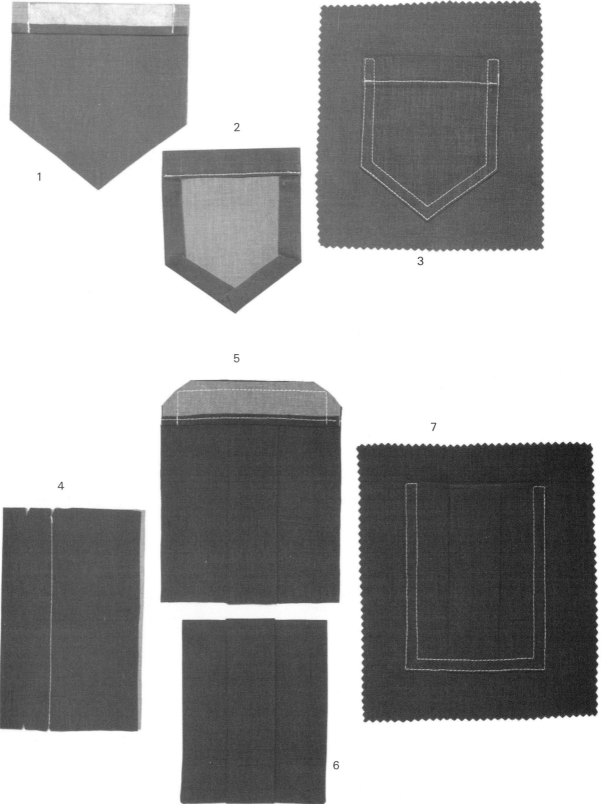

Patch pockets

Fig.1 Interface top turning, press up edge, and sew the ends.

Fig.2 Trim corners at top and turn through to wrong side. Press all turnings under, and stitch across top hem of pocket.

Fig.3 Lay on to pocket position marks on garment, and attach with two rows of topstitching.

Patch pocket with box pleat

Fig.4 Sew up back of pleat on right side.

Fig.5 Press box pleat and sew hem of facing. Face top edges.

Fig.6 Trim corners at top, and turn through to wrong side. Press all turnings under.

Fig.7 Lay on to pocket position marks on garment, and attach with two rows of topstitching.

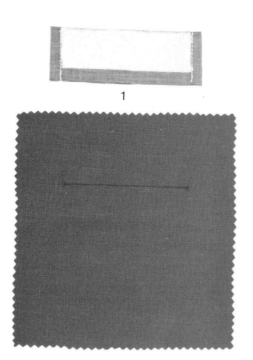

1

2

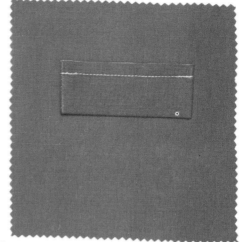

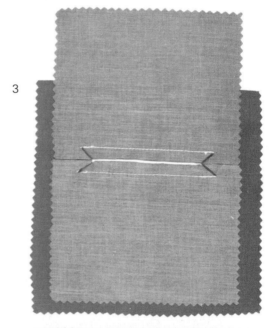

3

4

5

Welt pocket

Fig.1 Interface both sides of the welt, and sew ends. Mark pocket on right side and interface this area (see p.112, Fig.1).

Fig.2 Attach welt along pocket line.

Fig.3 Attach pocket bag, with lower row immediately over welt row of machining. The top row should be 1.5cm ($\frac{5}{8}$in) above, and slightly shorter at both ends than the first row.

Cut along the centre line and clip into the corners. Pull pocket through to wrong side and press.

Fig.4 Turn back to right side and lift up sides. Sew down the V to the pocket bag, and continue round the bag and through the other V.

Fig.5 Topstitch welt flap into place.

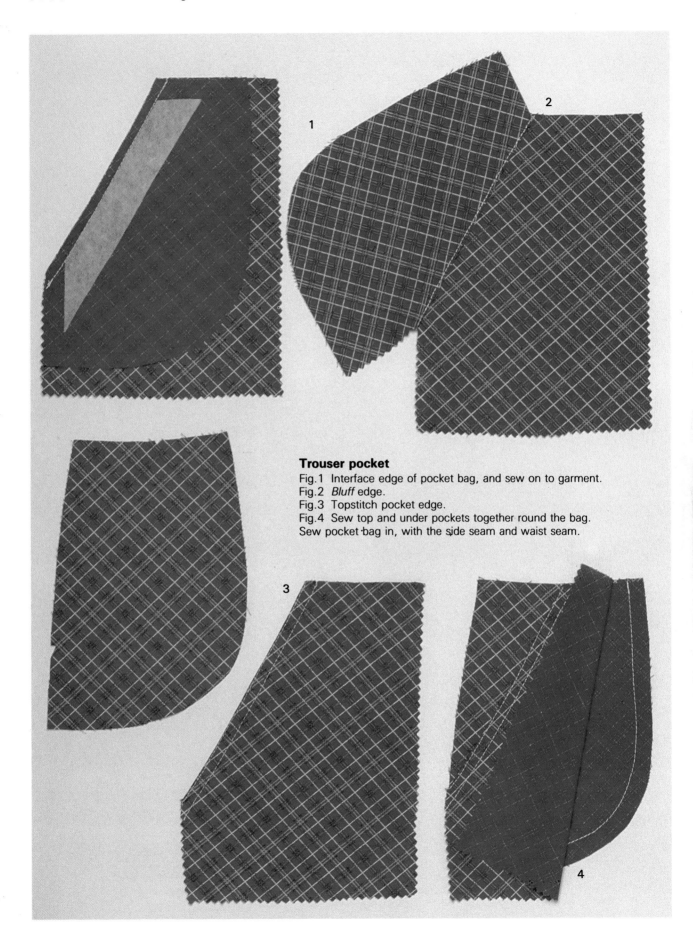

Trouser pocket
Fig.1 Interface edge of pocket bag, and sew on to garment.
Fig.2 *Bluff* edge.
Fig.3 Topstitch pocket edge.
Fig.4 Sew top and under pockets together round the bag.
Sew pocket bag in, with the side seam and waist seam.

Pocket and opening combined
Fig.1 Neaten open edges of pockets, and gather waist if part of the design.
Fig.2 Sew side seam, and round pocket bag. Clip into corner.
Fig.3 Press under front pocket at notch, and catch into waistband. Leave back pocket flap and continue waistband along it. Fasten with two buttonholes on this band, 6cm (2⅜in) apart. This opening can be used on one side or both sides of a skirt or trousers. If used on one side only, make sure the opening is big enough for the hips to pass through.

1

2

3

4

Cuff without opening

Fig.1 Machine two rows of gathering at end of sleeve, and pull up to circumference of cuff.

Fig.2 Interface cuff, overlock inside edge, and sew up seam. Press.

Fig.3 Sew up side seam of sleeve, and attach cuff to sleeve, right sides together.

Fig.4 Turn cuff up inside, and sink stitch through the seam, catching in the overlocked edge.

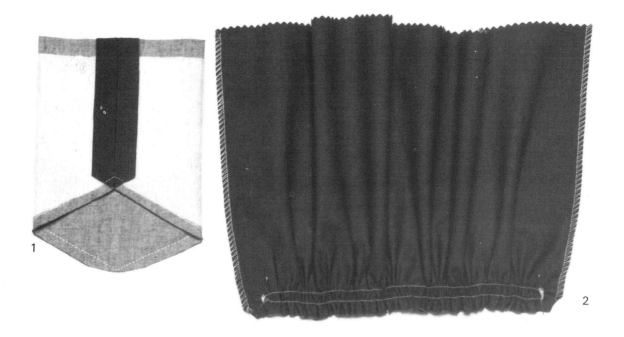

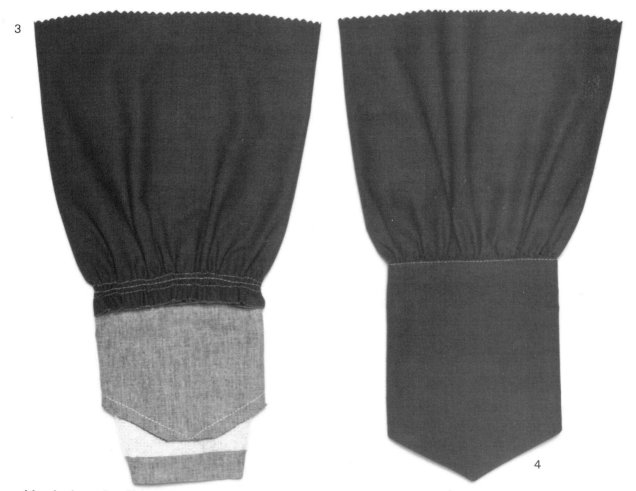

Turned-back shaped cuff

Fig. 1 Interface cuff and sew up seam. *Bag out* and trim corners.

Fig.2 Machine two rows of gathering at end of sleeve, and pull up to circumference of cuff.

Fig.3 Sew up side seam of sleeve. Attach under cuff (right side) to sleeve (wrong side).

Fig.4 Turn top cuff over to right side. Press turnings under and topstitch on to end of sleeve. Fold cuff up.

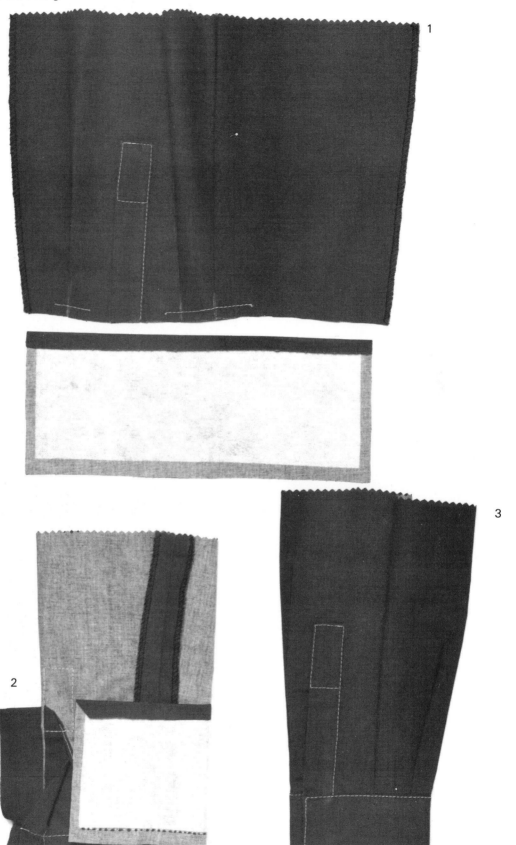

Shirt cuff with placket

Fig.1 Work placket (see p.100). Sew pleats. Interface cuff and press edge under.

Fig.2 Sew up sleeve seam and press.

Attach cuff to bottom of sleeve, on wrong side.

Fig.3 Sew ends of cuff, and trim corners. Turn sleeve to right side and topstitch cuff on to sleeve, continuing around outer edge. Add button and buttonhole.

Shirt cuff with opening in seam

Fig.1 Gather end of sleeve to fit cuff, not including extension. Interface cuff and press edge under. Attach cuff to sleeve, right sides together.

Fig.2 Turn right sides of cuff together, and sew the ends and the step together. Trim corners.

Fig.3 Turn cuff through to right side and press. Topstitch cuff on to sleeve, and continue round outer edge. Then sew up side seam from notch. Add button and buttonhole.

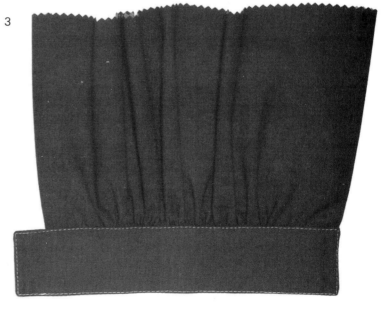

1

Sleeve with button and loop

Fig.1 Machine seams in sleeve, stopping the second seam at notch. Make and attach a *rouleau* loop to the front sleeve. Sew facing down to the notch.

Fig.2 Turn to the right side, and attach facing to hem and slit. Trim corners.

Fig.3 Turn facing under. Press and topstitch. Sew on button.

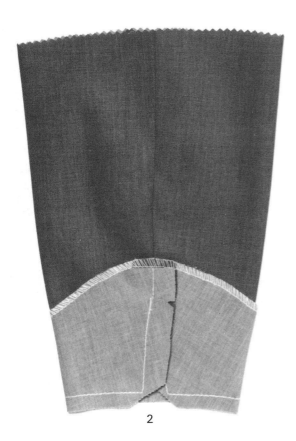

2

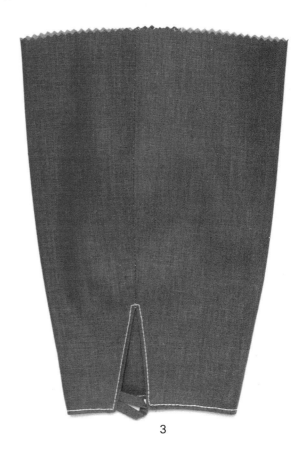

3

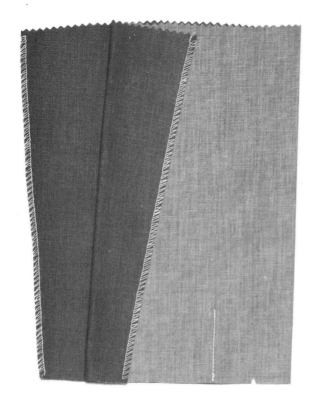

1

Sleeve with pleat

Fig.1 Sew pleat up to notch mark. Join seam on facing.
Fig.2 Press pleat in, and sew sleeve seam. Attach facing to sleeve.
Fig.3 *Bluff* facing edge, and catch facing up by hand in two places.
Fig.4 The finished sleeve with pleat.

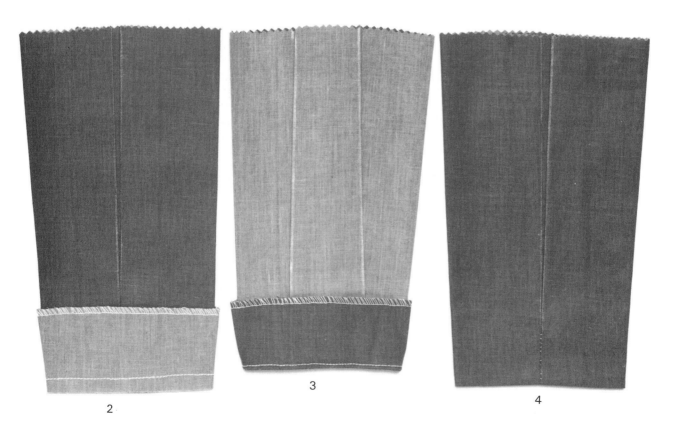

2

3

4

The Order of Making

The order of making will depend to some extent on the design of the particular garment, but the guidelines below should be followed as closely as possible.

The first series of points applies to all garments:

1 Press the fabric to be used, and pre-shrink if necessary.

2 Before laying the pattern on to the fabric make sure that the pattern is correctly marked with balance notches, grain lines, gathering notches, and dart and pocket positions. And of course that all the pieces fit together.

3 Place the pattern pieces in the most economical layout on the fabric (see p.76).

4 If the pattern does not include seam allowances allow room for them on the fabric and mark with chalk. Remember never to put seam allowances on iron-on interfacings.

5 Cut all the pieces out at the beginning, and have at hand the necessary sewing cottons, trimmings, buttons, zips, etc.

6 Snip all notches and mark with chalk the ends of darts, pleats, pocket positions, etc. There is no need to use tailor tacking.

7 Iron on all interfacings.

The skirt

8 Sew darts and press towards the centre.

9 Make up pockets, unless they are in the side seams. Press.

10 If there is a zip, sew the seam and then insert the zip while the garment is still flat. Press.

11 Attach pockets. Press.

12 Sew gathering, style seams, or pleats.

13 Join side seams, and side seam pockets. Press.

14 Make up the lining. Press darts away from the centre. Join the lining to the top of the skirt.

15 Make and attach hanger loops.

16 Sew on the waistband. Press.

17 Make all buttonholes and sew on buttons. If there are buttonholes on pocket flaps, do these before attaching the flaps to the skirt.

18 Turn up the hem and give a final press.

The shirt

8 Sew any darts, and press downwards or towards the centre.

9 Make up pockets, pocket flaps, epaulettes, and collars. Press.

10 Sew any gathers or pleats.

11 Attach the yoke to back and front. Press.

12 Sew sleeve plackets. Press.

13 Sew on pockets, pocket flaps, and epaulettes, and make front placket. Press.

14 Before joining up the side seams attach the collar, and sew on the neck and front facings.

15 With a loose-fitting shirt attach sleeve heads to the bodice, and then sew up the under sleeve seam and side seams of the shirt.

If the shirt is not loose-fitting join up the sleeve seams and the side seams of the shirt separately, and then set the sleeve into the armhole. Press.

16 Sew on the cuffs, unless the placket opening is in the sleeve seam itself. In this case attach the cuff while the sleeve is flat. Then sew up the seam of the sleeve. Press.

17 Make all buttonholes and sew on buttons. If there are buttonholes on the pocket flaps or epaulettes do these before attaching them to the shirt.

18 Machine up the hem and give a final press.

The trousers

8 Sew all darts and press towards the centre.

9 Make up pockets, unless they are in the side seams. Press.

10 If the zip is in the centre front, sew the front crotch seam from 4cm ($1\frac{1}{2}$in) below the zip mark to the zip mark.

11 Insert the zip.

12 Attach the pockets.

13 Sew any gathers or pleats.

14 Join the side seams, and make any side seam pockets.

15 Join inside leg seams.

16 Join the crotch seam, continuing from the 4cm ($1\frac{1}{2}$in) already sewn at the base of the zip, round to the centre back. Remember to sew two rows of machining at the back crotch to strengthen it. Press.

17 If the trousers have creases press them in before putting on the waistband.

18 Attach the waistband. Press.

19 Sew a buttonhole and button, and/or a trouser hook, at the front waistband.

20 Turn up the hems and give a final press.

Neatening Seams

Remember to neaten with overlocking or binding all seams that will show on the inside of the finished garment. This can be done before you start making up, with the exception of curved seams such as armholes or sleeve heads, which can stretch out of shape. Otherwise seams can be neatened as you go along. Never neaten a seam that is hidden, as this may cause unnecessary bulk.

Glossary of Terms

Appliqué A shaped piece (or pieces) of fabric, applied to the surface of a garment, for decorative effect.

Bagging out The stitching together of two pieces of fabric, right side inwards, around an outer edge, to form patch pockets and linings in jackets. A small gap is left (not at a corner), through which the fabric is turned.

Balance notch *(balance points)* A snip used on pattern pieces, and then transfered on to the fabric. The purpose is to help match up seams, so that they are sewn together at the right point, to keep the balance of the garment. Balance notches are also used to indicate ease, pleats or darts, and to show the width of a seam allowance.

Bar tack A row of machine buttonholing, approximately 1cm long, used to strengthen the corners of pockets and the tops of pleats.

Basque The part of a jacket or bodice that is below the waistline.

Beading The finished strips either side of a jet pocket.

Bias cutting A pattern piece cut at 45 degrees to the selvedge. The grain line is still placed parallel to the selvedge but is drawn on diagonally across the pattern.

Binding A double or single fold of bias fabric, used to bind and neaten the outer edges of a garment, or to neaten the edges of seams. A binding shows equally on both sides.

Buttonstand The extension from the centre line when the garment is to be fastened with buttons and buttonholes. The button must lie on the centre line, and the width of the buttonstand will be half the button diameter, plus 1cm ($\frac{3}{8}$in).

Costing The calculation of the exact quantities of fabric and trimmings (eg, buttons, zips, interfacing) required for a garment. A costing is used to price a garment either for manufacture or as a one-off.

Dolman A sleeve with the front part grown on to the front part of the bodice, and the back part grown on to the back part of the bodice. This allows the shoulder seam to continue down the centre of the sleeve. A gusset is often inserted under the arm for extra movement.

Ease The allowance made over and above the body measurements when making a pattern, to allow for movement.

Easing The joining of two pattern pieces, one of which is deliberately cut slightly longer, to give a little fullness when the two are joined. For example, a sleeve into an armhole.

Flare A pattern cut wider at one end than the other, to form a skirt when joined together.

Flaring Any main piece of pattern slashed open from the hem upwards until the opposite edge is almost reached, and then opened out to form a wider hem.

Fly A concealed opening consisting of a fold or flap, cut as part of the garment, to cover fastenings. For example, front opening on men's trousers, or on shirts, jackets, and coats.

Fusing The joining by heat of one fabric, usually an interfacing, to another. Fusible interfacings are bonded to the wrong side of the fabric by means of an adhesive layer that is melted by the heat of an iron.

Godet A segment, usually half or a quarter of a circle, that is added into a seam or slit to give a fluted look. One radius is joined to one of the sides of the seam or slit, the other radius to the other seam or slit. Godets were very popular in the long clinging dresses of the 1930s.

Grading The reducing or enlarging of the same design from the standard size pattern, to produce smaller or larger sizes of garment.

Grain The warp threads running parallel to the selvedge of the fabric. Every pattern piece must have a straight grain line marked on it, and when these pieces are pinned to the fabric the grain lines must be placed parallel to the selvedge.

Gusset A piece of material let into a garment to give more movement. A gusset is usually bias cut, and most commonly used at the underarm.

Lay A number of equal lengths of fabric, placed exactly on top of each other ready for mass cutting. The length of the lay depends on the length of the marker, which in turn depends on the length of the cutting table. In manufacturing industry as many as a hundred layers of fabric can be cut on one lay.

Marker A sheet of paper the same width as the piece of fabric to be cut, with all the pattern pieces drawn on it. The purpose of the marker is to get the tightest possible

arrangement of pieces, and so the most economical use of fabric.

In industry one marker may include pattern pieces of different sizes or even of different garments.

Mitre A technique for making neat corners. The turnings or bindings are folded so that they meet through the centre point, at 45 degrees to the corner.

Nap (or *Pile*) The surface given to certain fabrics whereby the fibres all lie in the same direction, for example face-cloth or velvet. With these fabrics the pattern pieces must be laid so that the nap on each is lying in the same direction. As a result the costings are usually higher.

Peplum A flounced, ruffled, or flared extension from the waistline to the hip line, used on jackets, blouses or dresses.

Pinking Cutting fabric with serrated shears to prevent the edges fraying, or to give a decorative effect to non-woven materials such as leather or felt.

Placket An opening in a garment to make it easier to put on and take off, whether at the sleeve, neck, or waistline. Plackets may or may not include fastenings.

Pleats Folds of fabric, either pressed or unpressed. There are six main types:

accordion pleats a regular zig-zag arrangement;

knife pleats folds lying flat and facing in one direction;

box pleats similar to knife pleats but with alternate folds facing backwards;

inverted pleats the reverse arrangement of box pleats;

graduated pleats knife pleats that are narrower at the waist than at the hem. They are governed by the waist and hip measurements;

sunray pleats all the pleats radiating from a half or quarter circle. The width of the pleats at the hem is governed by the length of the piece.

Accordion, graduated, and sunray pleats all require the use of a pleating machine.

Rouleau A bias-cut strip of fabric made into a tube by folding and machining it together on the wrong side, and then turning it through itself to the right side. Rouleaux can be used for decoration, as belts, or as button loops set into a seam in short lengths.

Scye The normal armhole of a garment.

Selvedge The finished edge running down each side of any length of woven fabric.

Shank (or *Stem*) The space between a button and the fabric it is attached to. The shank will vary according to the thickness of the fabric, to allow the garment to hang correctly when fastened.

Shirring Several parallel rows of gathering, made by machining with shirring elastic thread in the bobbin. It is most commonly used on cuffs and waistbands, or as an alternative to smocking on children's dresses.

Stay stitching A row of machining used to strengthen points that may weaken during wear. For example, at the neck point of a shawl collar.

Toile A prototype garment made up in calico or mull, that has either been designed and constructed on the stand, or made up from a pattern.

Tolerance (or *Ease*) The allowance made over and above the body measurements when making a pattern, to allow for movement.

Tuck A fold of fabric sewn parallel to the edge. A tuck can be any width, but when sewn very close to the edge is known as a pin tuck.

Underpressing Pressing done during the making up of a garment, when it is easier to reach parts before they have been joined together.

Vent An opening that does not fasten, usually in a seam. Vents are designed to allow extra movement, for example at the backs of jackets.

Wrap The extension from the centre line of a garment, that is added to make space for buttonholes.

Yoke A piece of garment fitted over the shoulders back and front, and joined to the rest of the garment in various configurations. A yoke is usually made in double thickness of material, to give extra strength.

Index

Main references;
illustrations and diagrams
numbered in **bold**.

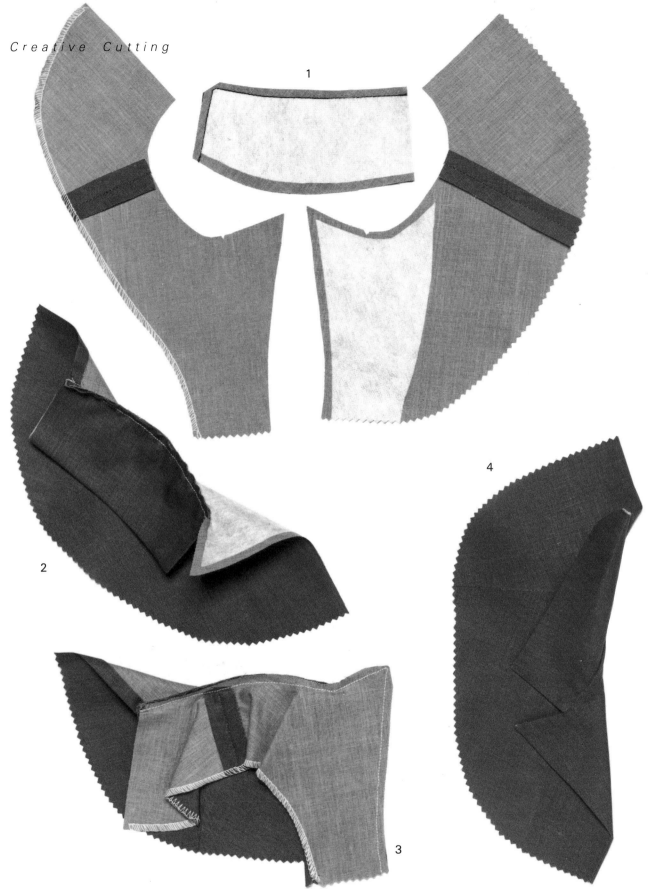

The rever collar

Fig.1 Interface under collar and rever on garment. *Bag out* collar (with a straight stitch across the point). Trim corners, turn to the right side, and press. Sew shoulder seams on garment and on facings.
Fig.2 Attach both edges of the collar to the right side of the neckline, as far as the notch.
Fig.3 Sew facings right side down to around outer edge. Trim corners, and clip back neck seam if necessary. If using a thick fabric layer the turnings.
Fig.4 Turn through to right side and press. *Gently* press in roll line.